W9-BQW-189

Programming Beyond Practices

Be More Than Just a Code Monkey

Gregory T. Brown

Beijing · Boston · Farnham · Sebastopol · Tokyo

Programming Beyond Practices

by Gregory T. Brown

Copyright © 2017 Gregory Brown. All rights reserved.

Printed in the United States of America.

Published by O'Reilly Media, Inc., 1005 Gravenstein Highway North, Sebastopol, CA 95472.

O'Reilly books may be purchased for educational, business, or sales promotional use. Online editions are also available for most titles (*http://safaribooksonline.com*). For more information, contact our corporate/institutional sales department: 800-998-9938 or *corporate@oreilly.com*.

Editors: Mike Loukides and Jeff Bleiel	**Indexer:** WordCo Indexing Services, Inc.
Production Editor: Kristen Brown	**Interior Designer:** David Futato
Copyeditor: Stephanie Morillo	**Cover Designer:** Karen Montgomery
Proofreader: Rachel Monaghan	**Illustrator:** Rebecca Demarest

October 2016:   First Edition

Revision History for the First Edition
2016-10-04:   First Release

See *http://oreilly.com/catalog/errata.csp?isbn=9781491943823* for release details.

978-1-491-94382-3

[LSI]

Table of Contents

About This Book

This is not a textbook. It is a collection of short stories meant to help you refine your way of thinking about and working on software projects.

You won't find any neatly packaged prescriptive advice within these pages. Instead, you will see example after example of the many problems we encounter as practicing developers, and the thought process involved in discovering how to solve them.

To encourage you to read this work in a way that brings out your creative side, I made you the main character in each of its stories. This will undoubtedly feel a bit weird to you, and even as I write this introduction, it feels weird to me, too!

My hope is that by embedding you in the work, this book can be more than just another stream of stern admonitions flowing down from the hilltops where Expert Programmers live. Instead, I want you to ask questions like, "If I were in this situation, would I really do things this way? If not, why not?"

As you read this book, I invite you to shine the light inward and question your own practices, habits, and perspectives at a deeper level. For best results, keep a journal nearby while reading and then share whatever ideas you jot down with your friends and coworkers. The concepts in this work are meant to be thought about and discussed, not just consumed.

In each story, you'll wear a different hat as you navigate your way through imaginary worlds that have been carefully constructed to teach you useful lessons. But the most important lesson of all will come from noticing the friction points and meaningful differences between the real you and the characters I've written for you.

Yes, that sounds a bit ambitious. But the entire point of reading or writing a book is to stretch ourselves a little bit, to become better at what we do. We're in this together, and with your help, I think we'll do just fine.

Buckle up, friend. It's time for our journey to begin.

The Journey

The story arc of this book covers a full career in software development, condensed down into a quick read that is meant to be accessible to all practicing developers.

Chapter 1: You are a competent programmer, and you are putting your skills to good use by helping people explore new product ideas through rapid prototyping.

Chapter 2: Your work becomes more complicated. You need to incrementally grow existing systems and you have many active customers to support. There's a feeling of conflict between what you think is the right way to work, and the pressure around you to ship new features quickly.

Chapter 3: You gain a deeper understanding of the costs of rushed decision making, especially at the integration points between your own code and the outside world. You've learned a great deal from past mistakes, and have started to focus on the complex relationships between business, customer service, and technical work.

Chapter 4: You are now a highly experienced developer. You are capable of helping others understand how to think about programming and problem solving, and have started to mentor a friend who is new to the field.

Chapter 5: You've become an effective teacher, and your development experience is strong enough that you're able to think on your feet, even in the context of live demonstrations. You use these skills to help students bridge the gap between theory and practice in a classroom setting.

Chapter 6: You are starting to progress down the path to mastery. You're able to pinpoint the weak spots of legacy software systems and design proper replacements for them, optimizing for both business outcomes and human-friendly workflows.

Chapter 7: You now have enough familiarity with the whole business of software that you're capable of working within an organization to identify and fix problems at every level. Your core competency is still in software development, but you've gained enough experience to communicate well at many levels.

Chapter 8: You start to wonder about the future of the computing industry as a whole. At this point, you're free to pick your own career path, so figuring out where you're going and why starts to be the most important question.

Because the career of a software developer is more like a spiral than a line, I encourage you to read through all of these chapters, no matter what your current skill level is.

I've written these stories to work at many levels, and there's no dividing line between the "basic" and "advanced" topics in this book. Each chapter is self-contained, so jumping around is alright...but for best results, read from cover to cover.

CHAPTER 1

Using Prototypes to Explore Project Ideas

Imagine that you work for an agency that helps clients navigate the early stages of product design and project planning.

No matter what problem space you are working in, the first step is always to get ideas out of a client's head and into the world as quickly as you possibly can. Conversations and wireframes can be useful for finding a starting point, but exploratory programming soon follows because words and pictures alone can only take you so far.

By getting working software into the mix early in the process, product design becomes an interactive collaboration. Fast feedback loops allow stumbling blocks to be quickly identified and dealt with before they can burn up too much time and energy in the later (and more expensive) stages of development.

There are many moving parts in even the most simple software systems, so it pays to set them in motion early on to discover how they interact with one another. In some ways every project is different, but in this sense every project is the same.

This week, you will work with your pairing partner Samara to develop a functional prototype of a music video recommendations system. The initial feature set does not need to be perfectly polished; it just needs to be useful enough to collect feedback from people who may find the product interesting.

In this chapter...

You will learn how exploratory programming techniques can be used to build and ship a meaningful proof of concept for a product idea within hours after development begins.

Start by understanding the needs behind the project

This music recommendations project is brand new, so you don't know at all what to expect yet. You get together with the client (Ross) for a quick chat to kick things off:

> **You:** Hi Ross! Thanks for meeting with me. My pairing partner (Samara) is listening in as well. We're ready to get started if you are.
>
> **Ross:** Yep, I'm ready. What's the first step?
>
> **You:** Well, first of all, I'd like to hear about what got you interested in music video recommendations. Knowing where an idea came from helps us figure out what to focus on in our prototypes.
>
> **Ross:** OK, sure. We've been running a blog where we post curated lists of music videos for a few years now. We have collaborators who specialize in building lists for many kinds of music, and people usually find our posts through organic search.
>
> Over the years, we've shared over 4,000 videos on our site. That's a massive library of music, but the only way to navigate it right now is one blog post at a time.
>
> We started to think through ideas on how to make our collection easier to explore. After considering some options, we decided that building some sort of recommendations system might be the way to go.
>
> The initial version can be simple, but we'd like to get something in front of a few dozen of our most active community members and blog contributors as soon as we can.
>
> **You:** Sounds like a great project! Let's dig in.

With the basic theme sorted out, you talk for a few more minutes with Ross about how to get a rough proof of concept put together. One question that often comes up in projects like this is whether the new work will be a standalone project or will need to integrate into some existing system.

In this case, Ross isn't entirely sure what he wants. But when you suggest that it might make sense to bring the question up later in order to focus all of the team's energy on figuring out whether the idea will even work, he agrees.

You talk through ways to make the prototype a bit more approachable to the readers of the music video blog and come up with a simple solution: use the blog itself to find the videos that'll serve as samples in the prototype. This way, the content within the new recommendations system will be familiar to both Ross and the readers of his blog, and there will be a clear connection between the new application and the original website even if they're technically operating in two totally separate codebases.

Use wireframes to set expectations about functionality

With a few of the big picture ideas sorted out, you shift your focus back to figuring out how to get started on the first iteration of the project. Wireframe diagrams are usually helpful at this stage, because they allow you to communicate the basic structure of what you're about to build, while creating a shared understanding of the work to be done—without getting bogged down in implementation details.

Rather than getting into a long discussion about different ways of implementing a recommendations system, you suggest starting with what might be "The Simplest Thing That Could Possibly Work."[1]

You: For our first attempt at a basic user interface, we might start with a page where the video player is displayed front and center. Underneath the player, there will be a few thumbnail images of recommended videos, which will be selected based on whatever is currently playing. Does that sound alright?

Ross: Sure, seems reasonable. I'll know better when I see it, though.

You: While we've been chatting, Samara has been working on a wireframe sketch that might serve as a good starting point. One second, I'll upload it...

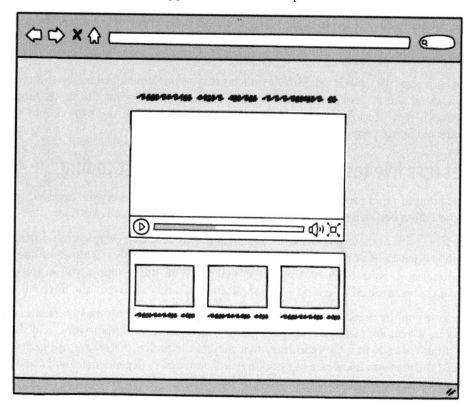

You: What do you think? We're trying to keep things as simple as possible to start with.

---

1 This idea from Ward Cunningham (*http://pbpbook.com/wardc*) serves as a reminder to focus on the goal that is driving your work, rather than getting lost in thoughts about imagined future costs and benefits.

Ross: That looks fine. It's similar to how I've seen video players work elsewhere on the Web, and that will probably make it easy for our users to understand it.

You: Great! Before we take our conversation any further, Samara and I would like to put together something similar to this sketch as an actual web page. We're just going to use placeholder images for everything, so this won't take us long, but it will help us test a few basic assumptions that will inform the rest of our work.

Ross: Sure, if you think that will help, go for it.

You are ready to dig in, but Samara appears to be lost in thought. When you ask her what's wrong, she explains that an idea for a better interface popped into her mind at the exact moment you asked Ross for feedback on her sketch.

Instead of the original workflow, Samara suggests building a player that would show a single video at a time with "thumbs up" and "thumbs down" buttons to allow viewers to indicate their preferences, and a single big "next video" button that would cause a new recommended video to begin playing immediately. This would be roughly similar to flipping through TV channels, but in a smart system that can guess what you might want to watch next.

This is a great idea, but it wouldn't be quite as easy to implement. After a brief discussion about the tradeoffs, Samara accepts the idea of trying out the more simple approach first, since it provides a faster path toward putting the project into the hands of the real people that might put it to good use.

Set up a live test system as soon as you start coding

The point of rapid prototyping is to reduce distance between everyone involved in a project: both between developer and client, and between client and customer.

To serve both of these purposes, having a running system that everyone can interact with is essential; it promotes trying things out rather than simply talking about them, and makes it easier to share progress as you go. With this in mind, you begin the usual chores involved in getting a web application up and running on the Internet.

Because you are using a decent application hosting platform, this mostly means setting up a generic "Hello World" page using your favorite web framework, and then pushing the code to a Git repository that detects the toolchain you are using. From there, the platform takes care of installing all the necessary dependencies and starting up a web server automatically.

Although it's running one of those weird URLs that looks like *baby-robot-pants-suit.somehostingprovider.com*, the application is live on the Internet within minutes.

At this stage, you have no clue what the production environment will end up looking like for the finished project and you don't really care. You're building exploratory features that serve the purpose of getting useful feedback from the client's target audience, and your code will be thrown away before the finished product ships anyway.

You cut every possible corner when it comes to infrastructure—you don't even set up a database system right away, because it's not yet clear whether one will be needed or not. Massive underinvestment is the name of the game here, and you manage to pull it off skillfully.

"Should we bother doing any sort of custom styling for this?" Samara asks.

You pause for a moment and think about it. But then you remember the YAGNI principle,[2] and the answer becomes clear.

"Nope. If the goal of this prototype was to make some sort of slick demo software for a marketing screencast, we'd want to focus on the looks from the get-go. But in this case, I think that Ross just wants to get this in front of a few of his friends to see what they think of it functionality-wise. On top of that, since this is a simple video playing application, the interface is going to be pretty minimal no matter what."

Samara seems convinced by your answer, even though you've once again chosen the expedient path over the elegant one. But you've worked together for long enough where this is just something you're both used to by now; there have been plenty of times where Samara has kept you from overthinking things, too.

You spend a few minutes wiring up the CSS framework you usually use while Samara pieces together some placeholder images. Once that work is done, you write some simple HTML to align the images in a grid layout with some hardcoded captions.

You spend just a little too long trying to figure out exactly where song titles should be placed and what size they should be. But then you remember two important points: none of those details matter right now, and it's time to get some lunch!

You deploy the code as-is, and a minute later the page is live on the Web:

---

2 You aren't gonna need it (YAGNI) (*http://pbpbook.com/yagni*)—A design principle that says functionality should not be added until it's truly necessary to do so.

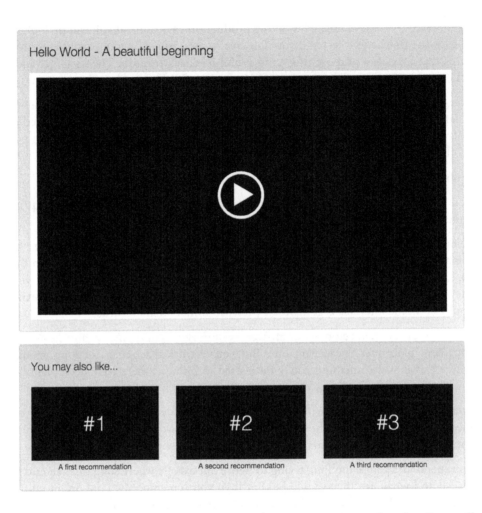

It really doesn't look like anything special, and you start to worry that the client will not understand why you might want to show him something this minimal.

To check your assumptions, you ask Samara what she thinks. She points out that not even the most simple things survive first contact with the customer, and that it would be better to ask for feedback too early than it would be to wait too long.

Feeling reassured, you remind yourself that the real goal of this first iteration is to set up a running system that will allow you to rapidly deploy new changes and kickstart the discovery process. From here on out, the client can directly interact with the software, and that will help you move a lot faster.

You send out a quick message to Ross letting him know that you have something ready for him to review, and you take a short break while waiting for a response.

Discuss all defects, but be pragmatic about repairs

When you return to your desk, you find feedback from Ross waiting for you:

> Hello developer friends!
>
> I just got the chance to try this out. On my laptop, the page looks pretty much like what you showed me in Samara's sketch, so no complaints there.
>
> I also tried to load the page on my phone, but things look awkward there. All of the videos take up the full width of the screen, and the recommendations are displayed in one long column rather than being shown side by side.
>
> We definitely don't need to make this thing look beautiful any time soon, but it seems like we should at least try to make sure all the recommendations are visible on a single screen, rather than having to scroll past a bunch of full-size videos.
>
> Is that something you think you can do something about?
>
> -Ross

As Samara predicted, something did manage to slip through the cracks, even in this extraordinarily simple first iteration. It's impossible to entirely guard yourself from making mistakes, but how you respond to them is critical.

You know that you can't leave the mobile UI question unanswered, but you don't want to dwell on it either. A reasonable response would be to draw up a fresh wireframe to communicate what the site should look like when rendered correctly.

Samara begins looking at a few popular video-based sites on her phone and finds that several of them use a common layout. She then sketches up something similar, but stripped down to the bare essentials.

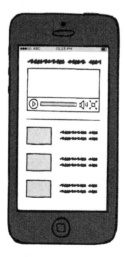

You send the wireframe along to Ross, and then spend a few moments talking over next steps with him:

> **Ross:** Thanks for the drawing! It looks like a decent starting point.
>
> **You:** That's great to hear. Now we have a decision to make: do we work on fixing the mobile layout issue right away, or do we put it off until later?
>
> Samara and I think that it may be worth implementing some useful recommendations functionality first, and then revisit UI questions down the line.
>
> That said, if you feel that a mobile-friendly design is essential even during the early stages of gathering feedback, we can take care of this before we move on.
>
> **Ross:** Is this kind of issue harder to fix later than it would be to deal with up front?
>
> **You:** I don't think so. Most of the work on the recommendations system will be under the hood, and so the desktop UI shouldn't need to change much. And if for some reason we do need to make major UI changes, we'd need to go back to the drawing board for the mobile sketches anyway.
>
> **Ross:** OK, let's wait a bit then. If any of our early testers complain about not being able to easily use this on their phones I may change my mind, but we can wait until we start collecting some feedback to worry about that.

Whenever you find a flaw in your software, it is tempting to drop what you're doing to work on repairs right away. But in the exploratory stages of a project, it's important to balance the cost of each defect you encounter with the cost of the time it might take to fix it.

In this particular case, time not spent on dealing with minor style tweaks on mobile is time that could be spent exploring the music video data sets and trying to come up with some recommendations rules. But by putting together a rough plan for how to fix the issue and communicating your ideas to the client, you eliminated some risks up front without having to invest a huge amount of effort.

Check your assumptions early and often

Early conversations with Ross have hinted that he is just trying to build something fun for his music community, a much easier problem to solve than "trying to create the most sophisticated predictive music playing service in the entire world!" or anything else along those lines.

However, it always pays to check assumptions on things like this as early in the process as possible. The initial wireframe sketches focused on what the UI for the application might look like, but now it is time to discuss how it should work:

You: Now I'll ask a more technical question…

What kind of rules should we use to implement recommendations?

Ross: Oh… hmm… I was hoping you might have some insights into that. Up until a few weeks ago, it didn't even occur to us that this project might be worth working on, so it isn't something we've done a ton of research on yet.

You: Well, there are a bunch of options here, ranging from basic category matching to very sophisticated approaches involving machine learning. It really depends, and although we could probably help you get a jump start no matter what, it isn't an area we specialize in.

Ross: I'm not sure if it's helpful, but our blog posts are all curated lists (e.g. "Ten great Miles Davis tunes you've probably never listened to," "A collection of live hip-hop performances from 1980s New York," "Family favorites for the Christmas season").

Our goal with this recommendations tool would be to help cut across these lists so that the listener can find other things they might like. So, for example, they might be listening to a 1980s hip-hop recording that was live in New York, and then we'd find other songs by that same artist, or we'd find other 1980s hip-hop songs, etc.

You: OK, this gives us something to think on, thanks. I think Samara and I might let these ideas percolate for a little while, and then we'll have more to show you sometime tomorrow. Does that sound good?

Ross: Absolutely! Thanks for the work so far; this was fun.

This conversation confirms that a simple recommendations system might be good enough and that Ross is flexible about its implementation details. You may have lucked out in this case, but if he had a more complicated idea in mind, it would have been better to find out sooner rather than later. So it never hurts to ask!

Limit the scope of your work as much as possible

Everything up until this point was just about finding an entry point into the project, but now it is time to roll up your sleeves and get some real work done. There are still plenty of unknowns to work out, and just studying Samara's original sketches for a few minutes generates many questions about implementation details:

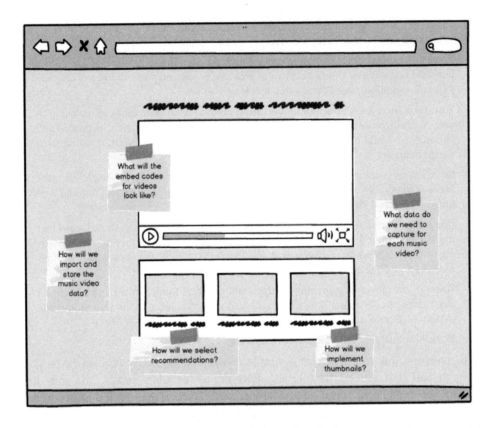

These questions crop up in a non-linear fashion, but before you can do any useful work, you'll need to prioritize them somehow.

Of the five important issues you and Samara have identified, two appear to be low-hanging fruits: how to generate embed codes for videos, and how to construct URLs for thumbnail images.

You pull up the music blog that Ross manages and check to see what video hosting service they're using. You also click through a few posts and check their source code to see how things are structured.

"Most posts use only embedded videos from FancyVideoService. The embed codes follow a standard format; the only thing that differs from video to video is its unique identifier."

"How about thumbnails? What do those look like?"

You hesitate for a moment, and then your clicking on various blog links intensifies, until you are convinced that you aren't getting anywhere.

"It doesn't look like they actually use thumbnails on their site. Everything I've seen so far is just embedded videos. So I guess we'll need to look that up."

You search the Web for a few minutes, but don't find any official documentation from FancyVideoService about how to grab thumbnails for their videos. You do, however, find a blog post that describes the URL format they use internally, and it's easy to generate these links using the same unique identifier that is used in video embed codes.

You manually create a few thumbnail URLs based on the videos from Ross's blog. They seem to work fine, although it is questionable whether this is actually a supported use case. For now, you hope for the best, but you'll need to get in touch with FancyVideoService to confirm that this approach is legitimate before the project wraps up.

With these chores out of the way, you can go back to the more subjective questions that came up when you were reviewing the mockup: what data to collect about each music video, how to go about storing that data, and how to use the data to generate useful recommendations behavior.

You and Samara start to talk through options, but then realize you're getting too far out into the weeds. So you go back to the classic question: "What is the simplest thing that could possibly work?"

After a few moments of quiet rumination, Samara gets a burst of inspiration.

"What if we started with artist matching? Based on whatever video is playing, randomly pick a few more songs by that same artist."

"Good idea. I think we'll need something more complicated before Ross sends this out for feedback, but I'm just really itching to get something on the screen that we can interact with right now."

Artist matching is an easy starting point, because all that is needed are video identifiers from FancyVideoService, song names, and artist names. If you grab a couple dozen songs from Ross's blog, that would be a decent sample data set to work with.

"What should we do about data storage? Should I go ahead and provision a—"

Samara abruptly cuts you off in the interest of keeping things simple.

"No need for that yet. Let's hardcode a sample data set as a bunch of arrays, and walk over those to generate the recommendations."

"You know that won't last us that long, right?"

"Doesn't matter. It doesn't have to!"

Samara is on a roll, so you ask her to do the coding while you piece together a handful of song names, artists, and video identifiers.

Fifteen minutes later, the two of you have something that looks halfway decent[3] running live in production:

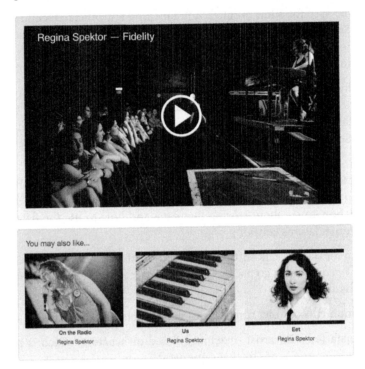

Just to show signs of progress and to hint at things to come, you drop one last note to Ross before wrapping up for the day:

You: Hey Ross, if you check out the website you'll see that we now have something up and running that kind of looks like a music recommendation system. It's very limited at the moment (only does artist matching), but thought it'd be fun to show you what we've been able to put together so far.

Ross: Whoa! Nice work. It definitely feels good to be able to interact with this rather than just looking at placeholder images, and it seems to be working mostly how I imagined it would in my mind.

I assume you'll be adding some more interesting recommendation behavior tomorrow? It doesn't need to be fancy, but it'd be nice to go beyond just artist matching.

---

3 Image sources: Piano (*http://pbpbook.com/piano*); Regina #1 (*http://pbpbook.com/reg1*); Regina #2 (*http://pbpbook.com/reg2*); Regina #3 (*http://pbpbook.com/reg3*)

You: Absolutely. We're still giving that some thought, but we will be in touch tomorrow with more to show you.

Ross: Great. Thanks again for working on this. I'm super pleased to see an early version of this idea take shape in the span of a single workday.

The basic *walking skeleton*[4] that you and Samara have put together will increasingly become more interesting to work with in future iterations.

While most of the first day of work consisted of getting the various moving parts into position, it has put you in a good place to begin exploring the real problem you are trying to solve. Had you attempted to jump straight into thinking about how to solve the full problem, it would have been harder to find a starting point, meaning much more stumbling along the way.

With not much time left on the clock for the day, you decide to spend the afternoon taking care of minor chores, reading blog posts, and using your phone to chase imaginary animals in exchange for imaginary Internet points.

Remember that prototypes are not production systems

After half an hour of quiet procrastination, Samara breaks the silence with some exciting news:

"Oh hey, customer support at FancyVideoService got back to us."

"They did? I didn't even know that you had emailed them. When did you do that?"

"While you were talking to Ross. I figured it'd be better to hear back about this sooner rather than later, but I'm surprised we got such a quick response."

You look over her shoulder to see what they had to say:

> Hi Samara,
>
> Hotlinking to the thumbnails for the videos we host is technically not against our policies, because we do want to be able to support a wide range of different use cases around sharing the videos we host.
>
> That said, it's not officially supported either, and there is no guarantee that the URL scheme will not change. We also reserve the right to deny access to anyone who seems to be abusing the service, at our sole discretion.
>
> A better solution would be to register for our developer network and then use the data APIs we provide. By looking up thumbnail URLs this way, your code will continue to work even if we make changes to the URL structure in future updates.

---

4 A walking skeleton (*http://pbpbook.com/skel*) is a small end-to-end implementation of a feature that gives you a starting point for thinking through and evolving the rest of the system it will eventually become a part of.

Another benefit of registering for the developer network is that if there is ever a situation in which your code unintentionally violates our service terms, we'll be able to identify you and send you proper notice about how to resolve the issues.

Hope that helps, and have a "Fancy" day!

-Sarah

You're relieved to find out that this feature is supported, even if the exact approach you took isn't what FancyVideoService prefers.

In the interest of saving time, you decide to stick with the unofficially supported way of generating thumbnail links for now, but you make a note about the issue so that whoever ends up building the production version of this software will know about it.

Happy with your progress, you call it quits for the day.

Design features that make collecting feedback easy

The next morning, you arrive at the office to see the whiteboards filled with a ton of notes that weren't there the night before. Curious about what Samara has been up to, you start to look them over.

"Oh wow! Ross will love this. What time did you get in this morning?"

"About an hour ago. I had this idea while eating breakfast, and decided to come in and start playing around with it."

Samara looks like she didn't get enough sleep, but you're so happy with her idea that you feel no need to mention that.

"So, should we get started on this then? I think it looks promising, and your notes are really, really good."

"Already done. Check the website."

You sit down and spend a couple minutes playing around with the new features. They are all working well, especially for a first major deliverable.

"How did you build this so quickly? I assume you cut some corners as we always do, but I doubt I'd be able to get that much done in an hour."

"Oh, you really do not want to see the code for this. You see all those recommendation scores? They're all being stored in a single browser cookie."

Figuring out the right balance of when to play fast and loose and when to tighten things up takes practice, but you trust Samara's judgment. You ping Ross to collect his feedback on the new functionality:

You: Hi Ross. I'm happy to say that we have something ready to show you whenever you're able to check it out. Just visit the website whenever you get a chance, and then I can walk you through what is going on there.

Ross: I'll take a look soon, thanks. I wasn't expecting to hear from you until at least lunchtime, so this is a pleasant surprise.

You: Here's a screenshot[5] that shows what things look like after viewing a bunch of videos. But definitely try it out yourself to get the full effect. :-)

Ross: Just spent a few minutes playing with the new feature. This is awesome!

One thing I noticed is the "interests" sidebar, which we never really talked about yesterday. Can you explain to me what that's meant to be used for?

You: Sure. It's worth mentioning up front that this sidebar isn't meant to be a permanent part of the application's interface.

Because the recommendation behavior is a little harder to explain than it is to see in action, we made this sidebar so that you can see how your tag scores are added up as you select videos in the application. Each tag is clickable, and whenever you click on a tag you will be sent to a randomly selected video in that category. You can use this to influence the scores and change the recommendation behavior.

Ross: Can you give me an example of how to try this out?

---

5 Image sources: Ella Fitzgerald (*http://pbpbook.com/ella*); Beck (*http://pbpbook.com/beck*); Thelonious Monk (*http://pbpbook.com/monk*); Regina Spektor (*http://pbpbook.com/reg2*)

You: Sure. Click "Thelonious Monk" a bunch of times, and see what happens.

Ross: Aha! As I did that, the recommendations for antifolk music started to become less frequent, and jazz recommendations become more frequent. Eventually, the system was offering me nothing but videos from Monk, which I guess is what was supposed to happen.

You: Yep. Do you feel like you understand this now?

Ross: I think I understand it well enough to want to play with it some more, and we may even be far enough along where I can send this to a few other people today and collect their feedback as well.

I am *really* glad you made that sidebar, though, because I would have had trouble understanding how the recommendations system worked based on your description alone. So thanks for that.

You: It was Samara's idea, and it's something we really should do more of. It helps you see a little bit of what's going on under the hood, and it gives you a chance to explore the rules we've implemented.

* * *

Ross: One more question before I send this out for feedback: where is the sample data coming from?

You: Right now, we're using a very small set of hand-picked videos based off of things we saw on your blog, but this is another area where we put in some effort to allow you to customize it yourself.

The system is currently set up to read its data from a CSV file, which you can edit in any spreadsheet software. Here, take a look at a few of the records that we currently have in the system:

q97xzziKqOl	Charlie Parker	Chasin' the bird	Jazz	1947
zre0u5XyNfY	Thelonious Monk	Round Midnight	Jazz	1944
oslMFOeFoLl	Dizzy Gillespie	Groovin' High	Jazz	1946
9KwLWpU0_K0	Ella Fitzgerald	How High the Moon	Jazz	1947
tHAhnJbGy9M	Regina Spektor	On the Radio	Antifolk	2006
fczPlmz-Vug	Regina Spektor	Us	Antifolk	2004
MMEpaVL_WsU	Regina Spektor	Eet	Antifolk	2009
4RJob0jSCX4	Regina Spektor	Dance Anthem of the 80s	Antifolk	2009
Z6XiO0o2R7M	Beck	It's All in your Mind	Antifolk	1995

You: The first column is the unique identifier for the video, which appears at the end of each FancyVideoService URL. The second column is the artist name, and the third column is the name of the song. Every column after that is treated as an arbitrary tag. Right now we have only two tags (genre and release year), but you can add as many of these as you want.

Ross: Wait…am I understanding this correctly? If you sent me this spreadsheet and I edited it to include any videos I wanted, you'd be able to directly import that and the videos would start showing up in the system with the tags I set?

You: Yes, that's the basic idea. We may need to be a little careful at first just because these things do need to be correctly formatted, but this is something we can help you with where needed.

What we had in mind here is that maybe you'd want to create a list of a couple hundred songs from your blog, and then that would give you a more realistic test of the existing recommendations behavior.

Once you've done that, we can definitely talk about ways to automate pulling your entire collection of 4,000 songs from your blog, but we figured that could probably wait until later.

Ross: This is great. I'm going to do exactly as you suggested, and put together a small list of songs based on the blog posts. After that, I'm going to make sure that at least a handful of people get to try this out today, and by the late afternoon I should be able to share their feedback with you. From there, we can figure out what to focus on next.

I can't thank you enough for putting this together. Really nice work.

You: This has been fun, and you've made our job very easy, so thank you, too.

Despite the feeling of mutual appreciation, it won't necessarily be smooth sailing from here. As the old saying goes, "the devil is in the details," and the next several iterations will get more detailed, probably stirring up at least one major unanticipated issue before you complete the prototyping phase.

But that isn't a sign of a flawed process; it's exactly what you should expect as a side effect of accelerated feedback loops. Prototypes can help you figure out how to build useful things faster, but they also help you fail faster. If you can spot a dead-end path before you've already spent a ton of time walking down it, it means you can spend more energy on figuring out where the right path is.

For the moment, though, both you and Samara are content to celebrate your early progress. A little bit of goodwill and trust built up in the early stages of a project can help build the kind of momentum that gets you through the inevitable rough patches that crop up in any creative work.

Recommendations and reminders

- Ask questions that reveal the goals of the people involved in a project. In doing so, you can both validate your assumptions and get more context on how other people see the problem.

- Use wireframes (rough sketches) to clearly communicate the basic structure of an application without getting bogged down in style details.

- Make sure to set up a live test system that everyone can interact with as soon as you start coding. The initial setup for this system needn't be production-ready; it just needs to be suitable for collecting useful feedback.

- In the early stages of a project, focus on the risky or unknown parts of your work. Prototyping is about exploring a problem space, not building a finished product.

Questions and exercises

Q1: The work on the music recommendations system in this chapter went fairly smoothly. What is something that could have gone wrong (but didn't) that would have made things much harder for the developers?

Q2: Pick two examples from the chapter where the developers chose to cut corners in order to work expediently. What tradeoffs were involved in those decisions? In other words, what did the developers give up to gain a bit of speed?

Q3: Imagine that instead of a simple recommendations system, the client had wanted a sophisticated implementation that made use of machine learning techniques. How would that change the direction of the prototyping phase for the project?

E1: Draw a couple wireframe diagrams describing the basic functionality of a wiki. Then repeat the process, but this time around sketch a different type of interface. Imagine the differences in implementation details between the two alternatives.

E2: Take any software tool or website you've used recently and pretend that you're about to implement it from scratch. Spend up to an hour or so exploring what your first steps might be.

Hey, you finished the first chapter! Awesome work.

Please enjoy this unrelated puzzle[6] as a token of my appreciation for your efforts.

>	22	#	6F	!	>	AF	#	CA	#	34	>	A9	>	A2	00
00	00	>	A1	00	00	#	34	00	42	42	00	42	FA	F2	FE
?	21	#	68	>	57	42	3D	FA	F2	FE	42	3D	87	00	87
00	00	>	A1	00	00	#	34	00	00	3D	FA	F2	FE	00	87
42	3D	FA	F2	FE	?	5A	00	87	?	17	00	87	FA	F2	FE
00	00	3D	3D	3D	00	42	00	3D	FA	F2	FE	87	#	00	?
42	3D	FA	F2	FE	42	3D	00	00	>	A1	00	00	#	34	00
31	21	00	21	21	#	65	#	6C	>	CC	21	FA	F2	FE	45
?	FA	F2	FE	?	02	00	00	>	A1	00	00	#	34	00	45
31	31	00	FA	F2	FE	?	17	FA	F2	FE	21	21	00	00	45
31	FA	F2	FE	00	00	00	00	>	A1	00	00	#	34	00	87
?	31	00	?	02	00	00	00	>	A1	00	00	#	34	00	FA
31	?	31	FA	00	FE	00	00	?	17	00	FA	#	6C	>	20
31	#	00	00	>	A1	00	00	#	34	00	#	FA	FA	F2	FE
FA	F2	FE	00	FA	00	00	?	17	00	FA	F2	FE	CF	?	FA
FA	F2	FE	00	00	>	A1	00	00	#	34	00	FA	00	?	00

Start at the beginning and end with a bang! Jump around if you must, but don't get lost in the noise. If you look carefully, you'll surely hash out what the hidden message is.

---

6 You won't need to write code to solve this problem, but an ASCII table will come in handy. Once you know the rules that govern this little Turing tarpit, a solution can be found in a few seconds with pen and paper.

CHAPTER 2

Spotting Hidden Dependencies in Incremental Changes

Imagine that you work for a product company that is known for their massive knowledge base of high-quality documentation.

The business is fortunate enough to have very dedicated customers, many of whom also write their own blog posts and articles to share helpful ideas on how to get the most out of your company's products.

To encourage the ongoing development of community-based learning materials, you've been asked to build a public wiki that will be hosted alongside the official knowledge base website.

You would prefer to implement this functionality as a standalone project, but for strategic reasons that haven't been fully explained, your product manager expects you to integrate the new wiki features into the existing knowledge base. The wiki will live in its own area, but it'll share the same codebase and infrastructure.

The challenge will be to bring the wiki online without having any negative impact on the existing website. On the surface this seems easy because no old code will need to be modified to support the new features, but deeper issues lurk below the waterline.

In this chapter...

You will learn about the many issues that can crop up whenever a production codebase is gradually extended to fit a new purpose.

There's no such thing as a standalone feature

You spend a couple days building out a minimal wiki, and the features you build end up looking quite similar to what exists within the knowledge base system. The only major difference between the two tools is that the original system is only used by a handful of trusted administrators, while this new wiki will be editable by anyone who visits your company's website.

To get some early feedback on your work, you show the wiki to Bill, your product manager. Bill spends three minutes playing around with it, and then turns to you and says, "This looks greaaaat. I'm gonna need you to get this shipped by Friday, OK?"

Rushing this new feature out the door seems like a terrible idea, but you try to make the best you can of a bad situation. You settle down and start to think through what could go wrong once this feature is live in production.

At first glance, it almost feels like there's not so much to worry about. The wiki lives in its own distinct section of the website, and you avoided modifying any of the code from the original content management system while adding this new feature set. Even if the wiki itself ends up crashing and burning, what is the worst that can happen to the rest of the website?

After a few moments, you notice something worth being concerned about: allowing anyone to create and edit pages without any restrictions is a huge risk from a storage standpoint.

There are many possible attack vectors to be concerned about, ranging from building huge documents to soak up storage capacity, to building tons of tiny documents, to building documents as quickly as possible to overload the storage mechanism itself.

Because both the knowledge base and the wiki use the same storage mechanism, an attack on the wiki could take the knowledge base down along with it. This is an example of an infrastructure-level dependency that isn't immediately obvious when you're looking at a newly introduced change to a codebase.

That idea leads you to notice another important point: the same web server hosts both tools. The conversion of Markdown to HTML for the wiki articles is handled in-process, and it's not especially performant. Someone wishing to disrupt the service wouldn't even need to wait until storage ran out; processing would grind to a halt as soon as the Markdown converter was overloaded with requests.

In light of these issues, you take a few steps to mitigate risks. They're nothing fancy, but they should help prevent a catastrophe:

- You limit the maximum number of pages to no more than 1,000 documents.

- You limit the size of each wiki page to no more than 500 kilobytes.

- You move the Markdown processing for the wiki into a work queue, and limit the queue size to 20 pending jobs, raising a "Please try again" error when the queue is overloaded.

- You add monitoring to track wiki page creation, deletion, and editing—and set up alerts for when these events are happening more frequently than you'd expect during ordinary operations.

- You add availability monitoring for the knowledge base website, pinging it twice per minute to ensure it is still accessible and responding within an acceptable amount of time. This should have been done long ago, but the clear need for improved monitoring makes this a perfect opportunity to add it in.

These measures on their own are not enough to make things completely safe. However, spending an hour to guard against the basic risks that come along with shared infrastructure dependencies is time well spent.

Confident that these changes have made your code much less dangerous, you let Bill know that the tool is ready to ship.

If two features share a screen, they depend on each other

A few weeks have gone by and the wiki has survived in production without any major headaches.

You were given a new project to work on immediately after the initial version shipped, and so it's been some time since you've had to even think about the wiki. But just this morning, you received an email from Sandi in marketing that will shift your attention back to it for a little while:

Hello programmer friend,

I'm not sure if you've been looking at the analytics dashboard for the wiki lately, but we're definitely seeing some growth in activity.

One thing I noticed when looking at the analytics data is that although we have almost 80 pages in the wiki, most people tend to only visit the articles that are directly linked from our most popular landing pages.

If it wouldn't be too much trouble, I'd like for you to spend a bit of time working on a new feature that will help customers explore the site.

What I'd like to see is a sidebar that lists the five most popular pages, the five newest pages, the five most recently updated pages, and five randomly selected pages.

We'd like to promote this new feature in our monthly newsletter, which will be sent out in the next couple days. So if you can sneak some time in to work on this before then, that would be excellent.

-Sandi

Adding this new sidebar is a reasonable request, and building it shouldn't be all that complicated. But as usual, it's something that you've been asked to do in a hurry, and that makes you nervous. *Will all this rushed work come back to bite you later?*

You could probably tell Sandi that you'd like a little more time to build out the feature, and that wouldn't create any massive problems for anyone. But before doing that, you decide to do a quick spike and see how far you can get in a single sitting.

Adding the new sidebar won't require modifying any existing behavior except for the UI for viewing wiki pages. In theory, this seems to be a low-risk change. In practice, you know there's no such thing.

Looking over Sandi's request, you realize that listing the five newest pages, the five most recently updated pages, and five random pages will be easy, because all of this information can easily be pulled with a simple database query. Determining the most popular pages is a more complicated task, so you put it off for now and focus on the low-hanging fruits.

You code up these simple queries and dump them into an ugly little sidebar on the right side of the wiki page. It takes about 20 minutes to cobble together, but it looks surprisingly functional. You wrap the whole thing in a feature flipper,[1] and make it so that the new sidebar will only be visible to developers. Two minutes later, the feature is live in production and you're ready to kick the tires.

The first time you visit the wiki, the sidebar looks like it's working perfectly. It is filled with a list of page links, along with a timestamp that indicates when each page was last updated.

After refreshing the page a couple more times, you hit your first problem: the page completely fails to load, and you get a generic "We're sorry, but something went wrong" page instead. This seemingly self-contained change managed to break the whole wiki!

You check your email inbox and sure enough, there's already an exception report waiting to be reviewed. You quickly discover the source of the problem: a handful of old records that had null values for their "last updated" timestamps, which were created before you started tracking update times.

This wasn't an issue until a few minutes ago, because those timestamps hadn't been displayed anywhere in the UI yet. The fix for this issue is easy: use the console to set any null timestamps to the date the wiki was rolled out, and then add a constraint to prevent records from being created with null timestamp fields in the future.

---

1 Feature flipping is a technique for rolling out features to a restricted set of users, whether it's an individual developer, a group of testers, or some percentage of real visitors to a website. Many open source libraries have been built to support this workflow, so finding one for your preferred programming language should be easy.

The lesson to be learned from this failure is that changes to database schemas always require some thought about data consistency. No matter how well isolated components are at the code level, there can still be hidden dependencies at the data layer. This means that a schema update that's meant to support a feature in one area of the codebase may break other seemingly unrelated features down the line—which is exactly what happened here.

You deploy a quick fix for the timestamp issue and then resume your therapeutic clicking of the browser refresh button. After half a dozen clicks you end up hitting another serious issue, but one that's very easy to fix.

You initially designed the sidebar to have a flexible width, with the idea that it would be allowed to expand a bit to accommodate longer page titles. But this is a half-baked idea that doesn't take into account the fact that one of the real wiki pages has the title "How to do something really amazing with the WidgetProFlexinator that you never thought was possible!"

By allowing the sidebar to expand to fit extremely long titles, the page contents themselves are stuffed into a tiny column that's completely unreadable. This is so silly that it's laughable, but it also serves as a useful reminder of another subtle dependency: if two features are displayed on the same page, you have to take steps to make sure they don't interfere with each other.

You set a maximum column width on the sidebar and redeploy. You hit the reload button until you're fairly confident that you've seen every single page in the wiki show up in the sidebar at least once. Things appear to be working fine.

You tweak the feature flipper configuration to enable the sidebar for Sandi's account, and you send her a quick email to let her know about your progress:

> Hi Sandi,
>
> I need to spend some time thinking about the "most popular" list, but we've rolled out an experimental sidebar with everything else you asked for. It's only visible to you and the development team for now, but please try it out and let us know what you think.
>
> -Your humble programmer friend

Within an hour after receiving Sandi's email, you've not only delivered something that she can give feedback on, but you also found and fixed a minor data consistency bug. Feeling satisfied with your progress, you take a break and go out for a walk.

Avoid non-essential real-time data synchronization

When you return to the office, a response from Sandi is already waiting for you:

> Hi there!
>
> Functionally, the sidebar looks very close to what we need. Two quick notes, though:
>
> 1. The "most popular" list is pretty important, because right now people mostly land on the wiki through organic search or via links to specific pages that get shared on social media. Even though these pages get a lot of visits individually, there currently isn't anything linking them together and we'd like to fix that.
>
> 2. Can you pick any color scheme for the sidebar other than "light brown text on an electric green background?" My own preference would be to match the look and feel of the sidebars from the knowledge base pages, but anything that doesn't burn the eyes would be an improvement. :-P
>
> Any chance you can take care of these issues and ship by Thursday?
>
> -Sandi

You often make work-in-progress features a bit rough on purpose to prevent others from thinking they're ready to ship, but she has a point—electric green is a step too far. Before moving on, you take a few minutes to roll out an updated version of the code that replaces the intentionally hideous color scheme with something that looks similar to the knowledge base styling, as Sandi suggested.

You start to think through the popularity ranking feature. To implement it, you'll need to pull down data from the site's analytics service. This could be done in real time through a search for the top 5 most visited pages in a specific time period, but this would result in an API call every time a wiki page loaded, which seems pretty wasteful. Even worse, this approach would unnecessarily introduce a hard dependency on an external service.

Your past experience has taught you that external service integrations are often full of headaches, because they can fail in all sorts of weird and unpleasant ways. You have to assume with every service integration that it may be slow to respond, it may reject requests due to rate limiting issues, it may have periods of downtime, it may return empty responses or incorrectly formatted responses, or it may trigger timeout errors —and if none of those things end up happening, it may still find some other way to ruin your day sooner or later.

If there was a genuine need to work with real-time data, you'd have no choice but to invest time and energy into writing robust, fault-tolerant code. But in this case, the popularity ranking would still be reasonably accurate if you simply updated the page visitor counts a few times per day. For that reason, writing a minimal script that will be run as a scheduled job is probably the right approach here.

You write a script that connects to the analytics API, looks up the stats for each page, and then imports the total visitor count for each page into the application's database. This script will be run by cron every four hours, and if any sort of error occurs or if it fails to complete its task within a reasonable time frame, you'll be notified. But for the most part, there's no real consequence to intermittent failures because this code will be running outside of the main application. The worst that can happen upon failure is that the popularity rankings become slightly out of date.

By taking this approach, you've reduced the scope of the problem in the application itself to another simple database query, making it no more complicated to implement than the "new pages" and "recently updated pages" features. You've also sidestepped the need to add further configuration information or libraries to the main web application, because your script runs in a separate standalone process and only shares information via the database layer.

Putting all these pieces together takes a couple hours, but by the end of the day you have the functionally complete feature running in production. Sandi takes one more look at it and lets you know that it looks good to her, so you roll it out to a small number of the wiki visitors and check to make sure that nothing bad happens.

After you're reasonably convinced that the sidebar is working properly, you set aside some time to clean up the code and put it through a proper review before it is officially announced on Thursday. Once that work is done, you roll the change out to everyone. By the start of the following week, Sandi is able to see some interesting changes in the analytics data that indicate that the feature is actually doing what she hoped it would.

Look for problems when code is reused in a new context

It has been three months since you last touched the wiki, and it has been working great for the most part. But today, all of that will change in an instant.

You arrive in the office to find Bill nervously pacing back and forth while talking on the phone. You can only hear one side of the conversation, but it's obvious that there is something seriously wrong.

"No, of course the wiki isn't sponsored by an herbal supplement company! We're not running any sort of advertisements at all."

"No, super-cheap-pills-for-you.com isn't a domain the company owns."

"No, we're not trying to pull some sort of practical joke, nor are we trying to damage the reputation of the company. I really can't believe you're even suggesting that."

"When did you first get a complaint about this problem? Just this morning? OK, that's good news. We'll stop the line and get working on a fix right away."

Bill ends the call and sits down next to you. He starts trying to explain what is happening, but you're already one step ahead of him.

"I pulled up the wiki as soon as you mentioned herbal supplements," you say. "It looks like we've got a major issue here: we're allowing <script> tags and who knows what else in the Markdown files. I'm working on a patch now that will temporarily redirect the entire wiki to a maintenance page, until we can assess the damages."

As soon as the maintenance page is up, you begin working on a script to detect the presence of HTML tags in the Markdown documents. This will help determine just how many pages have been affected, and what to do about it.

The report reveals that of the 150 pages that currently exist in the wiki, 32 pages use at least some inline HTML. But of those, only 12 of them are using the <script> tag. This could have been a lot worse if the issue hadn't been caught so quickly.

You generate a comprehensive list of links to match this report, breaking them into three groups: "No HTML," "HTML without script tags," and "HTML with script tags." Bill clicks through the "No HTML" links while you work on the others.

Every single page with a <script> tag on it illustrates the same behavior. It shows a modal window that says, "One moment while we redirect you to our sponsor's website…," and then it redirects the visitor to super-cheap-pills-for-you.com. This is incredibly irritating, but at least it seems like this is a single incident of abuse rather than a rampant problem.

For all of the documents that are using HTML tags other than <script>, there doesn't appear to be anything evil going on. Most uses of HTML appear to be from contributors who don't fully understand the Markdown format and instead stick to using the basic HTML tags that they're already familiar with. A handful of pages use HTML for more elaborate purposes, like displaying tables or embedding videos from other websites. The embed codes remind you that <iframe> is another tag that could potentially be used for abuse, but at least so far that hasn't happened.

Bill finishes auditing the Markdown-only documents and doesn't find any obvious signs of abuse. At this point, the wiki has been rejecting all incoming traffic for about half an hour, but you now have a much better understanding of the problem.

You start working on restoring partial functionality to the wiki to minimize negative customer impact. You first strip the <script> tags from the dozen documents that were infected with them, and then you deploy some code that allows read-only access to the wiki pages. Bill calls the customer support team to notify them about your progress, and for the moment it seems that tensions have eased as a result.

With the immediate crisis averted, you can now start dealing with the underlying cause of the problem: a Markdown processor that might have worked fine for a handful of trusted administrators, but isn't safe for use by random bots on the Internet.

At its root, this is another hidden dependency issue. You reused a tool that was reasonably configured for one purpose, without considering how that configuration might be harmful when applied in a slightly different context. In doing so, you focused on the superficial similarities of the two use cases rather than their fundamental differences, and that clouded your judgment. This is an example of bad code sharing practices, and it is something to learn from.

Going a bit deeper, the more subtle issue is that by not explicitly disallowing or restricting HTML tags from the start, you implicitly allowed for their use. This undefined behavior led contributors to believe this was an officially supported feature, even though it's clearly a defect from your perspective.

There is no question that the underlying security risks must be dealt with; it is essential to prevent anonymous visitors from injecting arbitrary JavaScript code into wiki pages. However, you also need to minimize the damaging effects of your repair.

After thinking about the issue, you decide that stripping all HTML tags is not the way to go. Although they represent a small percentage of the total number of pages in the wiki, some of the most popular articles make use of HTML in interesting ways that would be permanently broken by such a coarse-grained change.

You look into HTML sanitizing libraries and eventually find something that's fit for this purpose: it strips away any `<script>` tags, restricts `<iframe>` tags to a whitelist of specific trusted domains, and takes care of other edge cases that might cause issues.

To assess the impact of this change on the existing documents, you compare the raw HTML output from the Markdown processor to the sanitized output for each page. Most of the documents are unmodified by the sanitization process, leaving only five pages that need to be manually edited before the new rules can be applied.

To make sure that this particular issue never happens again without being noticed, you spend the rest of the afternoon writing tests for all the nefarious examples you can think of. This gives you some amount of satisfaction, but you worry that this won't be the last case of abuse you'll ever need to deal with on this wiki project. And that lingering thought keeps you on edge, even as you close up shop for the day.

Recommendations and reminders

- Don't assume that a change is backward-compatible or safe just because it doesn't explicitly modify existing features. Instead, be on the lookout for hidden dependencies in even the most simple updates.

- Pay attention to the many shared resources that live outside your own codebase: storage mechanisms, processing capacity, databases, external services, libraries, user interfaces, etc. These tools form a "hidden dependency web" that can propagate side effects and failures between seemingly unrelated application features.

- Make use of constraints and validations to help prevent local failures from causing global side effects where you can. But also make sure to have good monitoring in place so that unexpected system failures are quickly noticed and dealt with.

- Watch out for context switches when reusing existing tools and resources. Any changes in scale, performance expectations, or privacy levels can lead to dangerous problems if they aren't carefully thought out.

Questions and exercises

Q1: What about hidden dependencies (e.g., shared resources, services, and infrastructure) makes them harder to spot than the explicit dependency relationships between modules/functions in a codebase? What can you do to make them more visible?

Q2: Many of the examples in this chapter involved simple security flaws. Try to think of at least one other potential way a real wiki might be exploited[2] in the wild. Does your imaginary attack involve a hidden dependency in some way?

E1: Look through 10–15 resolved bugs in your own projects, and identify any that were at least caused in part by problems with hidden dependencies. Create a checklist to help catch similar issues in future code reviews.

E2: Choose one codebase that you're familiar with and list out a handful of the different features it supports. Then sketch out a hidden dependency web that shows the shared resources between each of the features.

---

2 See "CWE/SANS TOP 25 Most Dangerous Programming Errors" (*http://pbpbook.com/sans*) for some extra context.

CHAPTER 3

Identifying the Pain Points of Service Integrations

Imagine that you run an educational journal for programmers that has paying customers but is too small to support full-time work.

Together with your friend Huan, you maintain a custom web application that supports the journal and its subscribers. Built on a tight budget, the project mostly consists of glue code around common open source tools combined with a handful of web service integrations.

Over the years, you've started to learn that there are considerable costs and risks involved in using code that isn't under your own control. You've been bitten several times by action at a distance that wasn't accounted for when designing your software, and consequently you're now more cautious when integrating with external services.

As part of an annual retrospective, you will meet with Huan today to look back on a few of the biggest pain points you've had with third-party software integrations.

You've made a promise to each other not to turn this discussion into a game of "Who is to blame?", a perspective that can easily generate more heat than light. Instead, you will focus on guarding against similar problems in future work, and if possible, preventing them from occurring in the first place.

In this chapter...

You will learn some of the various ways that third-party systems can cause failures, as well as how flawed thinking about service integrations can lead to bad decision making.

Plan for trouble when your needs are off the beaten path

"How about we start by talking through the bracket stripping issue?" Huan asks with some hesitation. Immediately, your face turns red.

This issue is truly embarrassing, but it did teach you some important lessons the hard way. Now is as good a time as any to reflect upon it.

What exactly was the bracket stripping issue? It was a mistaken assumption that plain-text emails sent via a third-party newsletter service would be delivered without any modifications to their contents whatsoever.

A handful of test emails and a cursory review of the service's documentation didn't raise any red flags. But upon testing the second email you planned to send out, you noticed that all occurrences of the [] character sequence were silently deleted from the message.

This is a subtle problem, one that would have minimal impact (if any) on emails that didn't contain special characters. But because the emails you were delivering had code samples in them, any sort of text transformations were problematic. The fact that the [] character sequence appeared often in code samples made things much worse.

You contacted customer support to find out if they could fix the problem. Their response, summed up: "Yes, this problem exists, and we can't fix it easily because this strange behavior is fundamentally baked into our email delivery infrastructure."

One suggested workaround was inserting a space between the opening and closing brackets, which worked for *some* use cases, but not all. There were some situations where you really did need to have the exact [] character sequence; otherwise, code samples would fail with hard-to-spot syntax errors whenever someone attempted to copy and run them.

As a result, the newsletter service could not be used for sending full-text emails, so you changed up the plan and decided to host the articles on the Web. This is when Huan joined the project (there was no way you could build out the web application you needed and write articles for the journal at the same time).

Looking back, this kind of rushed decision making could have been prevented.

Had the flaw in the newsletter service been discovered before it was rolled out to paying customers, you wouldn't have been in such a hurry to find a workaround.

As you try to think through what you could have done differently, you struggle to come up with anything. You let Huan know you're drawing a blank, and ask her what she thinks could have been done better.

She suggests it might have been a good idea to do an email delivery smoke test: "Take a big corpus of sample articles and run them through the service to make sure they rendered as expected. This would have likely caught the bracket stripping issue, and wouldn't have cost much to build."

Her suggestion is a good one, but something about it makes you uneasy. You ask yourself why you *didn't* think to do something along those lines in the first place. That gets the gears turning in your head, and you start to see the flawed thought process that got you stuck in this mess to begin with:

> **You:** A smoke test would definitely have helped, but it never occurred to me that it was necessary. And that was the real problem.
>
> In theory, we should be approaching every third-party system with distrust until it is proven to be reliable. In practice, time and money constraints often cause us to drive faster than our headlights can see.
>
> **Huan:** So you're saying that you ran into problems because you rushed into using a particular solution without carefully evaluating it?
>
> **You:** Well, it's pretty clear that I was looking for a shortcut. So I chose a newsletter service based on its reputation. This sounds like a reasonable way of evaluating options quickly, but it isn't.
>
> **Huan:** But if the service was so popular, doesn't that count for something? I feel like I could have just as easily made the same assumption.
>
> **You:** Do you know that great burger shop down the street from here? The one everyone is always raving about as if it's the best place ever?
>
> **Huan:** SuperFunBurger! I *love* SuperFunBurger. Where are you going with this?
>
> **You:** What do you think about their fish sandwiches?
>
> **Huan:** Dunno. Never had them. Didn't even know they were on the menu, to be honest. Everyone always goes there for the burgers.

Because Huan is used to your way of talking in cheesy riddles, she has no trouble deciphering your main point: in the case of this particular newsletter service, you ordered a fish sandwich, not a burger.

With this issue laid out plainly on the table, you spend a few minutes talking through what could have been done differently:

- You could have searched around more to see if others were using the service in the way you planned to use it. It probably would have been hard to find similar examples to your own use case, and that alone would have triggered some warning bells that would have caused you to slow down a bit.

- It wasn't safe to treat this uncommon use case as if it would have just worked. Instead, it would have been better to treat it with the same level of uncertainty as any other source of unknowns. Noticing the risks would have caused you to write more comprehensive tests, and might have led you to consider running a private beta for at least a few weeks before allowing open signups.

- The other critical question that was never asked was "what do we do if this service doesn't work as expected?"—a question that should probably be asked about *any* important dependency in a software system. Even if you treated it as a pure thought experiment rather than as a way of developing a solid backup plan, asking that question would have left you less surprised when things did fail, and better prepared to respond to the problem.

Remember that external services might change or die

For your next case study, you talk about the time the site's login system suddenly stopped working, which caught both you and Huan by surprise.

In a weird way, this story relates to the email newsletter issue that you just worked through. The original plan was to deliver articles directly into a subscriber's inbox so that they could begin reading right away without any extra steps required. Changing this plan complicated things a bit.

Because the problems with the newsletter service caused you to move the articles into a web application—and because you were publishing materials that were meant to be shared with members only—you needed to implement an authentication scheme.

Forcing subscribers to remember a username and password would have been a bad experience, so you opted to use an authentication provider that most subscribers already used daily. This made it possible to share members-only links without subscribers having to remember yet another set of login credentials.

Setting up this feature was painless, and after initial development, you never needed to think about it at all. That is, until the day you tried to send out the 35th issue of your publication and received dozens of email alerts from the application's exception reporting system.

You were able to get a quick fix out within an hour of seeing the first failure, but your immediate response was predictably incomplete. You then implemented a more comprehensive fix, but that patch introduced a subtle error, which you only found out about a few days later.

The technical reasons for this failure aren't especially interesting, but you suspect that identifying the weak spots that allowed the problem to happen in the first place will generate some useful insights. To uncover some answers about that, you suggest playing a game of Five Whys.[1]

---

1 The Five Whys technique (*http://pbpbook.com/5whys*) is used to explore root causes for problems by repeatedly asking *Why* to reveal the broader context of an issue. Because most issues don't have a single root cause, the exercise can be repeated as many times as needed to explore different angles.

Huan agrees to play the role of investigator and begins her line of questioning:

Why did the authentication system suddenly fail?

The application depended on a library that used an old version of the authentication provider's API, which was eventually discontinued. As soon as the provider turned off that API, the login feature was completely broken.

Why were you using an outdated client library?

Authentication was one of the first features implemented in the web application and it worked without any complications. From there forward, that code was totally invisible in day-to-day development work.

No one ever considered the possibility that the underlying API would be discontinued, let alone without getting some sort of explicit notification in advance.

Why did you assume the API would never be discontinued?

The client library worked fine at the time it was integrated, and no one raised concerns about the implementation details or the policies of the service it wrapped.

When this feature was developed, no careful thought was given to the differences between integrating with a third-party library and a third-party web service.

An outdated third-party library will continue to work forever—as long as incompatible changes aren't introduced into a codebase and its supporting infrastructure. Because of the limited budget, the maintenance policy for the project was to only update libraries when it was absolutely necessary to do so (for things like security patches and other major problems).

A web service is an entirely different sort of dependency. Because a service dependency necessarily involves interaction with a remote system that isn't under your control, it can potentially change or be discontinued at any time. This wasn't considered in the project's maintenance plan.

To the extent this issue was given any thought at all, it was assumed that due to the popularity of the service providing the authentication API, users would be notified if the provider ever decided to make a breaking change or discontinue their APIs.

Why did you assume the API provider would notify its users?

In retrospect, it's obvious that every company sets its own policies, and unless an explanation of how service changes will be communicated is clearly documented, it isn't safe to assume you'll be emailed about breaking changes.

That said, there was another complication that obfuscated things. The client library used in the application wasn't maintained by the authentication service provider themselves, but instead was built by a third party. It was already an API version behind at the time it was integrated, and from the service provider's perspective, the tool was a legacy client.

The company that provided the authentication service also had an awkward way of announcing changes, which consisted of a handful of blog posts mixed in with hundreds of others on unrelated topics, and a Twitter account that was only created long after several of their APIs were deprecated. If we had researched how to get notified up front, we would have been better prepared to handle service changes before they could negatively impact our customers.

Why didn't you research how to get notified about service changes as soon as you built the authentication feature?

This feature was built immediately after the problematic integration with the email newsletter service, and it was thrown together in a hurry as an alternative way to get articles out to subscribers without delays in the publication schedule.

There were hundreds of decisions to make, and none of the work being done under that pressure was carefully considered. In a more relaxed setting, it would have been easy to learn a lesson from the newsletter service problems: third-party systems are not inherently trustworthy, even if they're popular.

But in that moment, there was still some degree of confidence that third-party services would work without problems, now and forever. And the only real explanation for that line of thinking is a lack of practical experience with service-related failures.

After completing her investigation, Huan concludes that it would be a good idea to audit all of your active projects to see what services they depend upon, and figure out how to be notified about changes for each of them. The two of you agree to set aside some time to work on that soon and continue on with your discussion.

Look for outdated mocks in tests when services change

Although the formal "Five Whys" exercise dug up some interesting points, it didn't tell the complete story of what went wrong and why. After continued discussion around the topic, you realize that—once again—flawed testing strategies were partially to blame for your problems.

It was easy to spot both the immediate cause of the authentication failure and the solution, because you were just one of many people who had been relying on the deprecated APIs. A web search revealed that an upgrade to your API client was needed—a seemingly straightforward fix.

Knowing it wouldn't be safe to update an important library without some test coverage, you spot-checked the application's acceptance test suite and saw that it had decent coverage around authentication—both for success and failure cases.

Feeling encouraged by the presence of those tests, and seeing that the suite was still passing after the library was updated—you assumed that you had gotten lucky and that no code changes were needed when upgrading the client library. Manually testing first in development and then in production gave you even more confidence that things were running smoothly.

A couple days later, an exception report related to the authentication service proved you wrong. It was clear the tests had missed something important. Or at least, that's the imaginary version of the story you somehow managed to remember in detail many months after it happened.

* * *

You dig through the project's commit logs to confirm your story, and sure enough, find an update to the mock objects in response to the final round of failures. You mention this to Huan, who doesn't appear surprised.

"That's absolutely right," she says. "We should have had some sort of live test against the real API. Because we didn't, our tests were never doing as much for us as we thought they were. And if we had a live test that ran before each announcement email, we might have caught this issue before it impacted our customers."

Your gut reaction tells you that Huan is probably right, but hindsight is 20/20 and testing isn't cheap.

That said, it would have paid to dig deeper when you spot-checked the test coverage. The mock objects were wired up at a low level, so the acceptance tests looked identical with or without mocks. Because of this, it was easy to forget they were even there.

After upgrading the library and seeing no test failures, and then checking that things were working as expected via manual testing, you assumed that you'd be in the clear. The automated tests would catch any unexpected changes in the client library's interface, and the manual test would verify that the service itself was working.

For the common use case of subscriber logins, this approach toward testing worked fine, meaning the first fix you rolled out after upgrading the client library did solve the problem for existing customers. It took a few more days to notice that the fix was incomplete; when a new customer tried to sign up, the authentication system kicked up an error.

This was a subtle problem. To complete authentication for an existing subscriber, all that was needed was the unique identifier that corresponded to user records in the database. When creating new accounts, however, you also needed to access an email address provided in the service's response data.

Upon the upgrade, the data schema had changed, but only for the detailed metadata about the user; the identifier was still in the same place with the same name. For this reason, active subscribers were able to sign in just fine, but new signups were broken until the code was updated to use the new data schema.

Turning this over a few times in your head, you can't help but acknowledge Huan's point about the importance of live testing:

> **You:** You're absolutely right; testing the real authentication service would have helped. But I also wish that I had been more careful when auditing our test coverage.
>
> **Huan:** What would you have done differently?
>
> **You:** I wouldn't just look at the tests; I'd also check the code supporting them.
>
> This would have led me to the configuration file where we mocked out the response data from the authentication service. And if I saw that file, I would have probably wondered whether or not it needed to be modified when we upgraded.
>
> **Huan:** Sure, that's a good idea, too. In the future, let's try to both catch these issues in code review by looking for outdated mocks whenever a service dependency changes, and also having at least minimal automated tests running against the services themselves on a regular schedule.
>
> **You:** Sounds like a plan!

Expect maintenance headaches from poorly coded robots

For the final discussion topic of the day, Huan suggests discussing something that initially appears to be a bit of a tangent: a situation where a web crawler was triggering hundreds of email alerts within the span of a few minutes.

As you think about the problem, you begin to see why she suggested it: on the open Internet, you don't need to just worry about your own integrations, it's also essential to pay attention to the uninvited guests who integrate with *you*.

You do a quick archaeological dig through old emails, tickets, and commits to reconstruct a rough sequence of events related to the problem:

- An initial flood of exception reports hit your inbox at 3:41 AM on a Wednesday. You happened to be awake, and immediately blacklisted the IP address of the crawler as a first step. Once things seemed to have settled down, you sent Huan an email asking her to investigate, and headed off to bed.

- When you woke up the next morning, Huan had already discovered the source of the problem and applied a two-line patch that appeared to resolve the issue. An incorrectly implemented query method was causing exceptions to be raised rather than allowing the server to respond gracefully with a 404 status code. This code path would be impossible to reach through ordinary use of the application; it was the result of a very strange request being made by the poorly coded web crawler that was hammering the server.

- At 4:16 AM on Friday, you saw a similar flood of exception reports. The specific error and IP address had changed, but the strange requests were an exact match to what you had seen on Wednesday. Although the crawler made hundreds of requests within the span of two minutes, it stopped after that. This is cold comfort, but it could have been worse.

- Toward the middle of the day on Friday, you pinged Huan for a status update but never heard back. By then, you had noticed that the problem most likely had come from a minor refactoring she had done after solving the original problem (which you hadn't even reviewed before the second email flood happened).

- At 6:24 AM on Sunday, the bot crawled the site for a third time, triggering the same flood of exceptions that you saw on Friday. At this point, you looked into the issue yourself and made a small fix. You also added a regression test that was directly based on kinds of requests the crawler was making, to ensure that the behavior wouldn't accidentally break in the future.

- On Monday, you traded some emails that clarified what went wrong, why it happened, and also what issues lurked deep beneath the surface that made this problem far more dangerous than it may have first appeared.

Reminiscing about this chain of events is uncomfortable. Seeing a problem happen not once, not twice, but *three times* is embarrassing, to say the least. It stings a bit to look back on these issues even though many months have passed.

You: I'm sorry for how I handled this one.

These emails make it sound like you messed up, but it's clear that my failure to communicate was mostly to blame.

Huan: Maybe that was part of it, but I could have been a bit more careful here, too.

I never thought about how the risks to the email delivery service tied into all of this, I just thought you were annoyed to keep getting spammed with alerts.

Your initial response was focused on the surface-level issue: your inbox was getting bombarded with lots of unhelpful email alerts, and that was a nuisance. These errors weren't even real failures that needed attention; they were the result of a bot doing things that no human would ever think to do.

Taking a higher-level view of the problem, what you had was an exposed endpoint in the application that could trigger the delivery of an unlimited amount of emails. To make matters worse, the email service you were using had a limited amount of send credits available per month, and each of these alert blasts was eating up those credits.

Upon closer investigation, you also noticed that the exception reporting mechanism was using the same email delivery service as the customer notification system. This was a bad design choice, which meant the potential for user impact as a result of this issue was significant.

Left untouched for a couple weeks, your monthly send credits probably would have been exhausted by these email floods. However, it's likely that you wouldn't have had to wait that long, because the system was delivering emails just as fast as the bot could make its requests. It is entirely possible that the service provider could have throttled or rejected requests as a result of repeatedly exceeding their rate limits.

This is yet another problem that could be chalked up in part to inexperience: the two of you had seen crawlers do some weird stuff, but neither of you had ever seen them negatively impact service before.

What your email history shows is that at some point you became aware of the potential problems but didn't explicitly communicate them to Huan. That wasn't obvious at the time; it only became clear after doing this retrospective today. This serves as a painful but helpful reminder that clear communication is what makes or breaks response efforts in emergency situations.

Remember that there are no purely internal concerns

You spend a few moments reviewing the retrospective notes from the email you wrote many months ago. It includes many useful thoughts that you and Huan have internalized by now:

- It's important to add regression tests for all discovered defects, no matter how small they seem.
- It's important to check for mock objects in test configurations so that you won't be lulled into a false sense of safety when a test suite passes even though the mocked-out API client is no longer working correctly.
- There are risks involved in sharing an email delivery mechanism between an exception reporting system and a customer notification system.
- It's worth looking into using a better exception reporter that rolls up similar failures rather than sending out an alert for each one.

These are all good ideas. It's a sign of progress that these bits of advice now seem obvious and have been put in place in most of your recent projects. But why weren't those issues considered in the first place? Why did it take a painful failure to draw attention to them?

You: I think that one common thread behind all of this stuff is that we had a well-intentioned but misguided maintenance process.

Huan: How so?

You: Well, I think the spirit of what we were trying to do was reasonable. We had agreed to treat customer-facing issues as a very high priority no matter how minor they were, and then freed up capacity to do that by underinvesting in some of the internal quality and stability issues.

Huan: So what's wrong with that? Isn't that what we still do? I thought this is one of those things you like to write about as if it were a good thing.

You pause for a moment. Then you finally find a way to put into words something that has been banging around in your head throughout this entire retrospective:

"Maybe there's no such thing as a purely internal concern. Maybe as long as our code talks to and interacts with the outside world, there will always be potential for customer impact when things aren't working as expected. If we pay more attention to what is happening at the boundaries of our system, and treat any issue that happens there as one worthy of careful attention, we'd probably get a better result."

The room falls silent for the first time in an hour. You let the dust settle for a few moments; then you and Huan head over to SuperFunBurger to try some of their wonderful fish sandwiches.

Recommendations and reminders

- Be cautious when depending on an external service for something other than what it is well known for. If you can't find many examples of others successfully using a service to solve similar problems to the ones you have, it is a sign that it may be at best unproven and at worst unsuitable for your needs.

- Remember the key difference between libraries and services: a library can only cause breaking changes if your codebase or supporting infrastructure is modified, but an external service can break or change behavior at any point in time.

- Watch out for outdated mock objects in tests whenever a change is made to a service dependency. To guard against potentially misleading test results, make sure that at least some of your tests run against the real services you depend upon.

- Use every code review as an opportunity for a mini-audit of service dependencies —for example, to evaluate testing strategy, to think through how failures will be handled, or to guard against misuse of resources.

Questions and exercises

Q1: The developers in this chapter struggle with bad behavior from a web crawling bot. What other sorts of problems can arise from uninvited guests integrating with your systems in ways you didn't expect?

Q2: Suppose there is a service integration that is essential to the core operations of your business: without it, everything grinds to a halt. How does this kind of dependency influence planning, testing, and maintenance strategies?

E1: Read through Richard Cooke's essay "How Complex Systems Fail" (*http://pbpbook.com/cooke*). Identify at least three of Cooke's observations that are relevant to the story in this chapter. Then try to find three others that describe issues you've encountered in your own work.

E2: Audit one of your production codebases to determine all of the external services it depends upon. Then think through what might go wrong if any of those integrations fail. Finally, write down whatever notes you can on how to reduce risks and make your software more resilient.

CHAPTER 4

Developing a Rigorous Approach Toward Problem Solving

Imagine that you have spent the last few months mentoring a friend who is in the early stages of a career in software development.

Your friend Emma started her first programming job about a year ago, and was mostly self-taught before then. Determined to gain experience as quickly as she can, Emma occasionally asks you for help whenever she hits a rough patch in her work.

In the last few weeks, Emma has noticed she seems to do well whenever she is working on well-defined tasks, but struggles when working on problems that have lots of fine-grained details that need to be sorted out before they can be solved.

Recognizing this stumbling block, Emma asks if it'd be worth trying out some programming puzzles as practice exercises.

You mull this idea over for a moment. Puzzles often needlessly complicate implementation details, represent data in inconvenient ways, and can be difficult to validate until all of their rules have been properly sorted out. This makes them awkward to use for developing practical coding skills, but perfect for exploring general problem solving techniques.

You find a puzzle you think Emma might like. She gets to work on it, while you stick around to help her out with any questions she has along the way.

In this chapter...

You will learn several straightforward tactics for breaking down and solving challenging problems in a methodical fashion.

Begin by gathering the facts and stating them plainly

Emma begins by reviewing the problem description for *Counting Cards*,[1] the puzzle the two of you will be working on today. She finishes reading it in five minutes, which surprises you. You ask her to share her thoughts on it:

Emma: I get the basic idea behind this puzzle, but I'm not sure how to get started.

You: That's OK. Try explaining what you know so far, and let's see how far that gets us.

Emma: There's a game transcript from some card game, and it lists out the different actions each player takes on their turn. You're supposed to track the flow of cards as the game progresses, in order to figure out what's in a particular player's hand at the end of each round.

You: Yep, that's my understanding of the problem, too. What do you think the challenging parts of solving it will be?

Emma: Well, you don't have full information about what cards are in play. So I guess you'd need to use some sort of process of elimination to figure out what is in everybody's hands? This is where I start drawing a blank.

You: Now that I think of it, this problem is probably complicated enough where just reading its description might not get us far. How about if we go back and take some notes on some of its key details, and see what that turns up?

Emma: If you think that would help, sure. Let's do it.

Sifting through the noise in order to find the signal is a necessary first step whenever you're working on a complicated problem. Rather then getting into a boring lecture on that topic, you attempt to demonstrate this to Emma by example.

You read the puzzle description out loud while she jots down notes, and then you swap roles and repeat the process. After you've finished reviewing and combining your notes, the basic details of the card game begin to take shape:

- The game is played with a single standard deck of playing cards.
- There are four kinds of actions that can happen on a player's turn: drawing a card, passing a card to another player, receiving a card from another player, or discarding a card.
- There is no apparent limit to the number of cards that can be drawn, passed, received, and discarded in a single player's turn.
- Once a card is discarded, it is out of play for the rest of the game.

---

1 *Counting Cards* (*http://pbpbook.com/cards*) by Eric Gjertsen. The chapter does not assume you've read this problem description, but if you want a more immersive experience, go ahead and do that now.

The game transcript lists out the various actions taken on each player's turn, but the amount of information provided varies for each player:

Rocky	Full information about all cards and actions.
Lil	Each turn lists several possible sequences of moves; you need to discover which of them is correct.
Shady + Danny	Publicly visible information only, i.e. you know if they draw, pass, or receive a card, but not what card it is. Discarded cards are visible to all, though.

The expected output for the puzzle is a list of the cards in Lil's hand at the end of each round. In order to generate this list, it'll be necessary to try out the various sequences of moves provided for each of her turns, and then figure out which sequence is the correct one. This is the process of elimination that Emma mentioned earlier; all that remains is to figure out how to implement it.

Emma takes a few minutes to look over her notes and think about the problem. Then, in a flash of insight, she finds a foothold that will be good enough to get started with:

> **Emma:** Oh, I see! If we track what we know about where each card is supposed to be, then we can eliminate sequences of moves that would lead to impossible outcomes... like when someone draws a card that has already been discarded, or attempts to pass a card that we know is actually in someone else's hand.

> **You:** Yep. It's worth noting that for the full challenge, the process of elimination won't be quite so straightforward, but your basic idea is exactly right.

> **Emma:** I think I need to study the problem a little more to understand where those complications might come up. But I've looked over some of the practice data sets for the puzzle and I think I understand them now. How about if we start with those and see how far I can get with what I already know?

> **You:** Sure! That sounds good.

Before this point, the problem description was just a sea of meaningless details and its input files were made up of cryptic symbols that resisted interpretation. But now with a sense of the end goal in mind and a glimpse of the path that might get her there, Emma sees the problem in a whole new light.

Work part of the problem by hand before writing code

You remain silent for a few moments while Emma reviews the first practice data set. This one is mostly meant to introduce the syntax and basic structure of the game transcript, so it only contains a single, valid sequence for each of Lil's turns:

```
Shady +?? +?? +?? +??
Rocky +QH +KD +8S +9C
Danny +?? +?? +?? +??
Lil +8H +9H +JS +6H
Shady -QD:discard -2S:discard
Rocky -KD:Shady +7H
Danny -QC:Rocky +?? +??
Lil -6H:Rocky -??:Shady -8H:discard +?? -10S:discard +??
* -JS:Shady +10S +QS
Shady +KD:Rocky +??:Lil -KD:discard -??:Lil
Rocky +QC:Danny +6H:Lil -9C:Danny -6H:discard -7H:discard +3D +3H
Danny +9C:Rocky -AD:discard +??
Lil +??:Shady +?? -??:Danny -??:Shady +??
* +AH:Shady +8D -8D:Danny -QS:Shady +8C
Shady +??:Lil -7S:discard +?? -10H:discard
Rocky -QH:Lil +5D -8S:Shady -3H:discard -QC:discard
Danny +??:Lil +?? +?? -??:Lil -3S:Rocky -??:Shady
Lil +QH:Rocky +??:Danny -AH:Rocky -QH:discard
* +4D:Danny
```

Ten minutes later, Emma breaks her focus and signals that she needs some help:

Emma: I'm having trouble figuring out how to process this file.

You: Do you mean you don't understand the actions themselves, or that you don't know how to write the code to parse the file?

Emma: The latter. For example, I know that things like +QH mean "draw a Queen of Hearts" and that -??:Shady means "pass an (unknown) card to Shady"—but I'm not really sure how best to model this data.

The format for the possible sequences on Lil's turn are a bit confusing to me, too. I know that the lines with the asterisks are meant to fill in the ?? parts of Lil's turn, but it's not obvious to me how to write the code to merge them together.

You: To be honest, I'm not sure how to model this data yet, either. I usually work through a problem manually for a bit before thinking about how to write the code; it helps to see the moving parts before getting bogged down in implementation details.

Let's do a step-by-step review of the game transcript, and see where that gets us.

Emma reads off the actions one by one, while you manually update a table that lists the state of each player's hand. After completing the initial draw and the first full round of play, you end up with the following table:

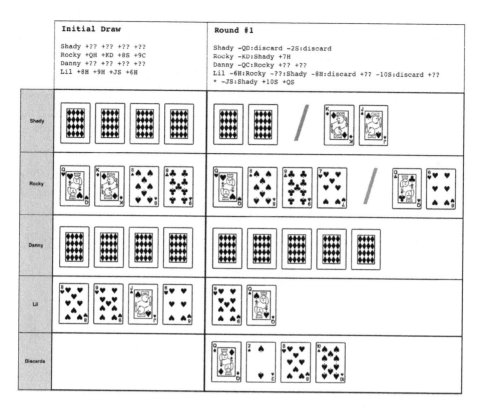

	Initial Draw	Round #1
	Shady +?? +?? +?? +?? Rocky +QH +KD +8S +9C Danny +?? +?? +?? +?? Lil +8H +9H +JS +6H	Shady -QD:discard -2S:discard Rocky -KD:Shady +7H Danny -QC:Rocky +?? +?? Lil -6H:Rocky -??:Shady -8H:discard +?? -10S:discard +?? * -JS:Shady +10S +QS

After you take a closer look at the table, the underlying structure of the problem becomes a bit easier to see:

- A hand is a collection of cards assigned to a player, sorted in insertion order.
- A hand may contain cards that have not been revealed yet.
- Passing cards is a two-step process that isn't finished until the receiver's turn.
- A discard pile is an append-only collection of revealed cards.

Using these basic ideas as a guide, Emma works on building some code to model the hand and discard pile concepts. She begins by writing some functions to match the various kinds of actions in the input files, so that something like +QC becomes `hand.add("QC")`.

In the process of coding up these models, Emma discovers that updating a player's hand involves more than just adding and removing elements from a collection. For example, the behavior of the `discard()` function depends on whether the card has been revealed yet or not, bringing up the question of how unrevealed cards ought to be modeled.

Several other small "gotchas" like this come up as Emma works and she starts to get frustrated. But when you remind her that working the problem by hand was only about figuring out the big picture ideas, she realizes that it's normal to hit some rough patches when sorting out fine-grained details in code.

Emma works through a few more edge cases that weren't easy to spot when working the problem by hand. Eventually, her code starts working as expected in isolated tests, so she manually translates the game transcript from the first sample data set into function calls on her models.

Emma runs her script and is pleasantly surprised when it produces the correct output on the first try. This small win is important because it will keep her motivated as she works through the rest of the puzzle.

Validate your input data before attempting to process it

Emma turns her attention to the second practice data set:

```
Lil +5C +2H +8H +6D
Shady +QH +AC +7C +2D +8C +3S -??:Lil
Rocky +KS
Danny +4H
discard +4D +7D +JS +6S +6H +2C +5D +3C
Lil +??:Shady -6D:discard -??:Danny +?? +??
* +8H:Shady -2H:Danny +JD +2D
* +8C:Shady -8C:Danny +JD +4S
* +QH:Shady -2H:Danny +7D +AS
* +AC:Shady -8H:Rocky +AS +8D
* +8C:Shady -2H:Danny +10H +9H +4C
* -8H:Danny +8C:Shady +4S +AS
```

Noticing the small differences between how this file is formatted and how the first sample file was laid out, she returns to the problem description to read the notes about what this sample is for:

```
This file represents one round of the game immediately before Lil's turn.
In this sample, you know what's currently in each of the players' hands and
what's in the discard pile. Here there are six possible branches, only one of
which can match Lil's actual moves. See if you can determine which is the
correct set of moves, and deduce the cards in Lil's hand at the
end of the round.

Note that the invalid branches in this sample cover many (but not all) of the
corner cases you're likely to encounter in the main puzzle.
```

Emma tells you that she plans to begin by walking through the transcript and listing out all the cards in play, similar to how you approached the first data set.

This is a good idea, but there is something else that is important to look at first. You ask her to review the branch syntax to make sure that she fully understands how it works before proceeding with her plan.

To test her assumptions, Emma constructs a table with the fully expanded turn instructions for each branch. In theory, this should just be a matter of matching up any action with a ?? to the corresponding action in each branch. In practice, it turns out that not all branches are properly formed:

Lil +??:Shady -6D:discard -??:Danny +?? +??		
+8H:Shady -2H:Danny +JD +2D	→	Lil +8H:Shady -6D:discard -2H:Danny +JD +2D
+8C:Shady -8C:Danny +JD +4S	→	Lil +8C:Shady -6D:discard -8C:Danny +JD +4S
+QH:Shady -2H:Danny +7D +AS	→	Lil +8H:Shady -6D:discard -2H:Danny +7D + AS
+AC:Shady -8H:Rocky +AS +8D	→	Doesn't match template! (passes to wrong player)
+8C:Shady -2H:Danny +10H +9H +4C	→	Doesn't match template! (draws three cards)
-8H:Danny +8C:Shady +4S +AS	→	Doesn't match template! (actions out of order)

Emma is surprised by this discovery. The two of you talk a bit about it because there is an important lesson to be learned here:

Emma: This feels like complication for the sake of complication. It doesn't really add anything to the interesting part of the problem, so why would the puzzle's author want us to jump through this extra hoop?

You: Well, I'd argue that it was most likely meant to make the puzzle a little more realistic. Raw data is usually messy, so the idea of having to process this sample before we can make use of it is only natural.

Emma: So are you saying that you knew the sample data would have problems, and that's why you had me hand-verify it?

You: No, it's just a good habit to get into; otherwise, you can easily write programs that take garbage in, and spit garbage out.

As soon as you identified a single branch that wasn't in the correct form, you discovered the need to validate *all* of the branches. It only took you a few minutes to find this issue, so it was well worth the initial time investment.

There are certain cases where assuming that data is in a valid format is a safe bet, but if in doubt, it's better to err on the side of caution.

Emma: OK, I think I understand that now, thanks.

In order to write a validation method, Emma needs to process Lil's turns and extract the actions with ?? in them. You suggest converting this data into an array of arrays, to capture its basic structure in code:

```
Lil +??:Shady -6D:discard -??:Danny +?? +??

[[:receive, "Shady"], [:pass,"Danny"], [:draw], [:draw]]
```

From here, the same translation can be applied to each of the branches. If doing so produces an identical structure, the branch is at least in the correct form. If it produces a different result, it can immediately be marked as invalid.

Emma walks through the six possible branches in the sample file and manually translates the lines of text into the format you suggested. In doing so, she finds that the first three exactly match the structure of Lil's turn, while the last three all produce non-matching structures.

Expected structure (+??:Shady -??:Danny +?? +??)

```
[[:receive, "Shady"], [:pass,"Danny"], [:draw], [:draw]]
```

Passes to wrong player (+AC:Shady -8H:Rocky +AS +8D)

```
[[:receive, "Shady"], [:pass, "Rocky"], [:draw], [:draw]]
                      ^^^^^^^^^^^^^^^^
```

Draws extra card (+8C:Shady -2H:Danny +10H +9H +4C)

```
[[:receive, "Shady"], [:pass, "Danny"], [:draw], [:draw], [:draw]]
                                                          ^^^^^^^
```

Actions out of order (-8H:Danny +8C:Shady +4S +AS)

```
[[:pass, "Danny"], [:receive, "Shady"], [:draw], [:draw]]
 ^^^^^^^^^^^^^^^^^^^^^^^^^^^^^^^^^^^^^^
```

The two of you work together to implement a validation method based on these ideas, and then use a similar approach to build a parser for the game transcripts. Emma learns some interesting text processing tricks along the way, but they're not the focus of the lesson. She quickly shifts her attention back to the problem at hand.

Make use of deductive reasoning to check your work

With the improperly formed branches weeded out, the next step will be to logically verify the three remaining branches to figure out which one lists the correct sequence of moves. At this point, a sketch of the state of each player's hand is exactly what's needed, so Emma puts one together:[2]

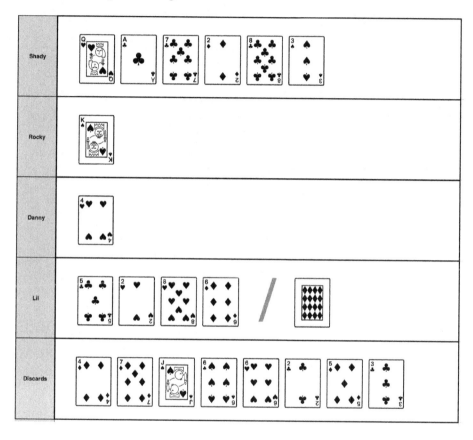

Using the table of moves she produced earlier, Emma walks through the branches one by one and hand-verifies them while talking out loud:

Emma: The first branch is `Lil +8H:Shady -6D:discard -2H:Danny +JD +2D`.

Right away, I can see this is impossible. Because Lil already had the Eight of Hearts in her hand, there is no way that Shady could pass it to her in this turn.

---

2 The state of everyone's hand is known with one exception: Shady passed a card to Lil, but that card has not been identified yet. That said, it must be one of the cards listed in Shady's row.

You: That's right! How about the next one?

Emma: The second branch is `Lil +8C:Shady -6D:discard -8C:Danny +JD +4S`.

Shady does have the Eight of Clubs, so there's no reason she couldn't pass it to Lil. Lil does have the Six of Diamonds, so discarding it would be a valid move. If Shady did pass the Eight of Clubs to Lil, then Lil could definitely pass it immediately to Danny, so no problems there either.

Finally, both the Jack of Diamonds and the Four of Spades don't appear in anyone's hand or in the discard pile, so there's no reason why Lil couldn't draw them from the deck. I'd say this branch is possible.

You: Sounds right to me. Because this data set only covers a single round of the game, we know (in theory) that the third and final branch is impossible without even looking at it. But just to check our work, we should verify it nonetheless.

Emma: OK, the third branch is `Lil +8H:Shady -6D:discard -2H:Danny +7D +AS`.

I see immediately that this has the same problem as the first branch; it's impossible for Shady to be passing the Eight of Hearts because it's already in Lil's hand.

You: Nice work; it looks like we've got our answer. Now it's time to move on from the practice data sets and start exploring the real challenge.

Author's note

In the process of constructing this dialogue, I had made a transcription error that incorrectly led me to believe the second branch was invalid. It wasn't until I wrote the "let's check just to be sure" line that I caught my error. Embarrassing, but a funny enough coincidence that proves the point of this section.

Solve simple problems to understand more difficult ones

Working with two practice data sets has given Emma a solid starting point for solving the puzzle, but the difficult part will be combining these ideas together in order to process a full game with many branches per round.

Before going any further, you check in with Emma to see what her plans are for the remaining work to be done:

You: Can you walk me through what you plan to do next?

Emma: Sure. The challenge data set is basically a combination of the two samples we've seen so far, right?

You: That's right. The first data set showed you what a transcript of game actions looked like, and from that you were able to start tracking everyone's hands as the game played out.

The second data set showed you how to narrow down the possible sets of actions on Lil's turn until you found the only branch that would not lead to an impossible move.

Emma: OK. I should update the code so that whenever we get to Lil's turn, we'll first eliminate any branches that aren't in the proper form.

From there, we take one branch at a time and run its sequence of actions. If we can run all the actions listed in the branch without running into an impossible move, we will know we found the right branch.

What I don't understand is why the challenge data set is so small. With only three possible branches for each round, and only five rounds to go through, wouldn't that at most require checking 15 different possibilities? That seems really easy to do by hand.

You: Nope, there are actually 243 different possibilities. To understand why, go ahead and check out the three branches for Lil's first round in the challenge data set. Use the same process of elimination we did earlier, and see where it gets you.

Emma reviews the first several lines of the challenge data set:

```
Shady +?? +?? +?? +??
Rocky +5S +QH +6H +JC
Danny +?? +?? +?? +??
Lil +7C +3S +8D +9H
Shady -4H:discard -??:Danny +??
Rocky +10D -10D:Danny +4S +2D -4S:discard -JC:Lil
Danny +??:Shady +10D:Rocky +?? +?? +?? -4D:discard
Lil +JC:Rocky +?? -??:Shady +??
*   +JH -7C:Shady +10C
*   +JH -8D:Shady +9S
*   +JH -8D:Shady +10C


(... next four rounds would follow here ..)
```

After scribbling notes down for a few minutes, Emma notices what you had hoped she would: without looking beyond the first round, it is impossible to eliminate any of the three branches listed for Lil's first turn.

When she does look ahead, Emma starts to see how a particular branch choice might lead to an impossible move on a future turn, but eliminating possibilities ends up taking much more effort than she originally thought it would. Discovering a dead end can mean playing out the game all the way to the last line of the transcript, making this data set much more difficult to process by hand than the practice sets were.

With this detail of the puzzle clarified, there is a whole lot more to think about. Emma takes a short break to process it all, while you think through how you might be able to help her get through this tricky part of the problem.

When Emma returns, you show her a simplified problem that you've constructed to help her understand the work that needs to be done:

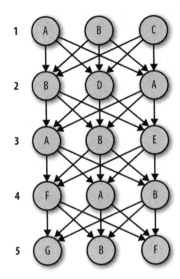

Emma: Wow, that's a lot of arrows! What am I looking at here?

You: Well, it's basically an idealized form of the *Counting Cards* puzzle. I know it looks a bit abstract, but I promise it is directly relevant to solving the problem.

It consists of five sets of letters. The goal of this puzzle-within-a-puzzle is to pick exactly one letter from each set so that you end up with {A, B, C, D, E} in the end. The order that you collect the letters in doesn't matter, so long as you pick up all five.

The arrows represent all the possible sequences of choices you could make if you were choosing letters blindly. It amounts to a total of 243 distinct paths from top to bottom.

Emma: Ah, I see what you did there. The five sets represent the five rounds of the card game, the three choices per set represent Lil's branching turns, and the 243 possibilities are all the different combinations that can be made of those branches.

Seeing the structure of the problem definitely helps, but I'm still a little lost on how to translate this into implementation details. Can you give me a few more hints?

You: Sure. Imagine that you don't know much about how everything in this graph is laid out, but you do know the goal: to get a set that (when sorted) is equal to {A, B, C, D, E}. From that, you can start to derive rules for when you know you're on a dead-end branch. Can you think of one?

Emma: I see some other letters in the sets, like F and G. If we ran into one of those, we'd know it wasn't a valid choice, and so we could eliminate the branch straightaway.

You: Yep, that's roughly similar to when we reject branches in the card game that don't match the structure of Lil's turn. Can you find another constraint that's more subtle?

Emma thinks for a few minutes, and then realizes that if you ever happen to pick the same letter from more than one set, it's impossible to produce the correct output. For example, if you chose the first elements of the first three sets, you'd end up with ABA. With only two sets left of letters to pick from, it'd be impossible to complete the full {A, B, C, D, E} set.

You point out the similarity between this observation and the idea of making an "impossible move" in the card game, and Emma smiles as she begins to understand what you're getting at.

> **You:** At this point, we've simplified the puzzle to a graph traversal problem. We use a selection criteria to identify dead-end branches, and we keep iterating until we find the one path that gets us all the way to the end.

> **Emma:** I understand the selection part, but I might need some help in figuring out how to iterate through the different paths.

> **You:** Well, the data set is small enough where it's probably not worth looking for some sort of fancy heuristic to narrow the search space. Instead, you could probably use a simple depth-first search.

> **Emma:** So you mean: keep taking the left-most path until you hit a dead end, then jump one level up and try the next path, repeating that over and over?

> **You:** Yep! Go ahead and look at the graph and tell me what the first few dead-end paths would look like.

> **Emma:** ABA, ABB, ABEF, ABEA, ABEB... Should I keep going?

> **You:** Nope. You've successfully exhausted the AB path. The next step would be to go on to AD and repeat the process, and so on from there.

> Now what I'd like you to do is write the program that solves this little puzzle. I can help you where needed, but it should be fairly straightforward.

It takes some effort, but Emma eventually gets her program up and running. When she's done, she has a script that recursively walks through the graph, trying out the various different paths.

Emma runs her program, and then traces the path it outputs onto the original graph, producing the following result:

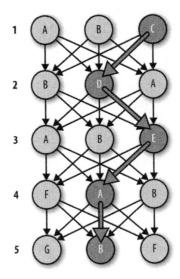

You: Awesome! You found the needle in the haystack. Now should we get back to the original puzzle and solve that too?

Emma: If you don't mind, I think I'd like to solve the rest of this on my own. The stuff you've showed me so far has been super helpful, and I think I can keep applying it to sort out the rest of the puzzle.

You: Hey, that's a great idea. I'm available to help if you need me, but as long as you're feeling up for it, finishing it on your own will almost certainly be more rewarding. It also reminds me of the most important lesson from what we worked on today...

Emma: What's that?

You: Real problem solving is often a solitary experience. You can get support from others, but in the end, you need to understand all the pieces of a problem for yourself in order to see how it all comes together. That's the essence of what it means to think rigorously anyway: to understand something with a great deal of precision and detail.

Emma: That makes a lot of sense. And it seems like if you can take complicated problems and break them down like we did today, they become more approachable. Before it kind of felt like hitting a wall whenever I started working on a problem that I didn't immediately understand, but I think I might be able to look at things differently now.

You: Really good to hear that. I won't lie, this is something that we all need to remind ourselves of from time to time. But it seems like you definitely have the right idea. Good luck with the rest of the puzzle!

As you pack up your things, you look over and see Emma still hard at work. A puzzle that she had initially thought was totally beyond her reach has captured her interest and attention, and now she has a great chance at solving it.

Recommendations and reminders

- The raw materials of a problem description are often a scattered array of prose, examples, and reference materials. Make sense of it all by writing your own notes, then strip away noise until you are left with just the essential details.

- Behind each new problem that you encounter, there is a collection of simple subproblems that you already know how to solve. Keep breaking things down into chunks until you start to recognize what the pieces are made of.

- Challenging problems are made up of many moving parts. To see how they fit together without getting bogged down in implementation details, work through partial solutions on paper before you begin writing code.

- A valid set of rules operating on an invalid data set can produce confusing results that are difficult to debug. Instead of assuming that input data is clean, avoid the "garbage in, garbage out" effect by validating any source data before processing it.

Questions and exercises

Q1: Think of an example from your own work where you had to apply a rigorous problem solving approach. What was something you got stuck on before finally solving the problem, and how did you end up getting unstuck?

Q2: There can be downsides to approaching problems in an extremely precise and methodical fashion. What are a few situations where a rigorous thought process can end up hurting more than it helps?

E1: Rigorous thinking is essential whenever you need to work with low-level, rigid, context-free rules. Read about the "Anatomy of Information in Software Systems" (*http://pbpbook.com/anat*) to see how these concepts apply in the design of file formats and protocols.

E2: Write a program that is capable of solving the {A, B, C, D, E} puzzle. Once you have it working, generate a new data set that is 26 levels deep, with 26 choices per level, and arrange it in such a way that there is only one unique path that passes through all of the letters in the alphabet. Are you able to process this new data set without modifying your program? If not, why not?

You've made it to the middle of the book. Hooray!

Here's another little riddle for you to solve, if you're up for it…

$	AF	$	DB	$	CE	$	8D	$	AA	$	87	$	37	$	B5
$	A2	$	87	$	64	$	37	$	6B	$	3D	$	1A	$	13
>	^	21	3F	AE	AC	C1	D2	24	15	#	66	>	^	00	00
00	#	68	>	^	D2	A9	10	16	41	00	00	00	AC	C1	D2
00	AC	C1	D2	24	00	#	67	>	^	00	00	00	00	00	?
00	?	21	29	25	24	00	AC	C1	D2	24	#	75	>	^	00
00	3F	AE	AC	00	00	21	29	25	24	00	00	3F	AE	AC	00
00	00	00	#	6E	>	^	00	#	20	>	^	00	00	00	00
00	?	D2	A9	10	16	41	00	00	00	00	00	AC	?	D2	24
00	00	00	00	21	3F	AE	AC	C1	D2	24	15	00	00	00	00
00	#	61	>	^	00	3F	AE	AC	00	#	79	>	^	00	00
00	D2	A9	10	16	41	#	69	>	^	00	00	00	#	3F	>
^	00	00	00	?	00	00	00	00	D2	A9	10	16	41	00	00
00	00	00	#	76	>	^	00	#	65	>	^	00	00	?	00
00	AC	C1	D2	24	3F	AE	AC	00	00	00	00	#	74	>	^
00	?	D2	A9	10	16	41	00	00	00	!	00	00	3F	AE	AC

Midway through the $tack, it's time to unwind. A secret message is what you'll find!

CHAPTER 5

Designing Software from the Bottom Up

Imagine that you are a visiting instructor in a software design course, and you hope to bridge the gap between theory and practice.

Your friend Nasir is responsible for running the course, and he asked you to come help out because he's only had mixed results so far.

When reviewing a case study, Nasir's students easily grasp the main ideas and they ask creative questions that lead to great conversations. But when it comes to applying design concepts in their own projects, most students struggle to make the connection.

The problem is that most of the students have not had much practical experience with building software systems. This lack of perspective leads them to view software design as an abstract exercise, rather than a concrete and essential skill set.

Textbook examples reinforce this viewpoint by demonstrating a top-down style where design ideas just spring out of the woodwork. Real design doesn't work that way, but students often assume it does and end up feeling discouraged.

To help reveal where design decisions come from in the first place, you will build out a small project in real time and discuss it with the class as you work. This way, the students will be able to take an active role in the iterative design process that goes along with building a system up brick by brick.

In this chapter...

You will learn a step-by-step approach to bottom-up software design, and examine the tradeoffs of this way of working.

Identify the nouns and verbs of your problem space

Nasir kicks off the class with a brief discussion of what you'll be building: a minimal simulation of a just-in-time production workflow.

Rather than leading in with theory, Nasir instead describes how just-in-time delivery has been used to make online shopping much more practical than it used to be:

- When a customer buys a product, it gets shipped to them within a day or two at the most, typically from a location within 100 miles of wherever they live.

- Inventory levels at local warehouses are kept to the absolute minimum necessary to prevent a product from going out of stock. Replenishment is done on a continuous basis; every time a local warehouse ships one of their products to a customer, a corresponding order is submitted to a larger fulfillment center.

- There is a constant flow of products from fulfillment centers to the local warehouses, so any item that needs to be replenished is just thrown onto the next truck, plane, or train headed to that location.

- Whenever inventory is shipped from a fulfillment center to a local warehouse, replenishment orders are automatically submitted to third-party vendors, many of whom also use a just-in-time production workflow to allow for ordering replacement products in small batches.

- Even though running the whole ordering process from end to end might take weeks, the flow of goods is set up in such a way that customers get their products shipped from a nearby location that effectively never runs out of stock, and manufacturers produce a number of units roughly comparable to the amount that actually get sold.

Under this model, products flow to where they need to be *just in time*, and this minimizes the amount of waste and waiting time throughout the whole production system. This way of working is common now but was considered a ground-breaking industrial innovation just a few decades ago.

Nasir lingers on that point for a moment, and then signals to you that it's time for the lesson to begin. Without missing a beat, you share a convenient anecdote that reveals some of the specifics what you'll be modeling today:

> **You:** My father worked on an assembly line all of his life, and saw his own company transition from a big batch process to a just-in-time workflow.
>
> **Student:** That must have been such a huge change! It seems like two totally different ways of doing things.
>
> **You:** Well, that's just the thing. It was a huge change in how the company operated at the business level, but at the production level it was an amazingly small change.

Before the transition, a crate of widgets would arrive from an upstream supplier, and workers would process them in some way before passing them downstream to the next station in the line.

When the company switched to just-in-time production, things pretty much stayed the same—with one small tweak. The flow was reversed so that new widgets were processed only when empty crates returned from downstream stations.

Student: So in other words, your dad knew to start working whenever the next station down the line needed more of whatever he was producing?

You: Yep! It wasn't obvious to see from any one station, but the whole thing was chained together that way: from the most simple parts at the start of the line to the finished product at the end.

Working backward from customer orders, the entire assembly line was able to determine exactly how many units to produce and when, without ever directly coordinating with anyone except for their immediate neighbors.

This is a process that has always fascinated me, because it shows how very interesting emergent behaviors can arise from seemingly simple building blocks. And for that reason, I thought it would be fun for us to model this behavior from scratch, and discuss some interesting software design principles along the way.

When Nasir asks the class if that story explained enough about the just-in-time production workflow to begin simulating it, they laugh nervously as if they can't tell whether he is joking or serious. But then he immediately follows up with a more manageable question: what were the important nouns and verbs in the story?

It takes a few minutes, but the students eventually identify many of the keywords that are relevant to the simulation, including *widget*, *crate*, *supplier*, *order*, and *produce*.

You then ask the students to take two of these words and combine them in a simple sentence that seems easy enough to implement. After a moment of quiet contemplation, one of the students shouts out a suggestion:

"I know! Let's build a crate and put a widget in it!"

This is a great place to start, so you thank the student for her idea, and get to work.

Begin by implementing a minimal slice of functionality

To begin your demonstration, you prepare some minimal UI elements to work with, consisting entirely of simple geometric shapes. You then wire up some basic logic, while the students watch you work.

Within a few minutes you have a small rectangle on the screen with a red circle in it, representing a rudimentary "widget in a crate."

When you press the space bar on your laptop, the circle disappears. When you tap it again, the circle reappears. You demonstrate this several times…probably a few more than necessary to make the point.

Regaining focus, you pull up a diagram that describes the API for the `Crate` object:

Crate

push(widget)
Adds a widget to crate

pop()
Removes widget from crate

isFull()
Returns *true* if crate cannot fit any more widgets, *false* otherwise

Empty Crate ☐   Full Crate ◉

In order to even get to this starting point, you had to make several design decisions. Subtle as they may be, these decisions will influence the rest of your design throughout the remainder of the project:

Nasir: As a quick recap of what you've done so far, there are now two objects in the system: crates and widgets. A crate is a container that can hold widgets, and it is possible for crates to be full. A widget is still mostly undefined, and I assume that it's meant to stand in for an arbitrary product of some sort?

You: That's right. Looking ahead a little bit, the thing I'm interested in modeling is how materials flow through a just-in-time production system—the actual contents being processed don't really matter. What does matter is the presence of these crates, because we'll be using those to determine whether new materials need to be produced or not.

Student: Oh, I think I see where this is going. You plan to make use of these crates in the same way they were used in your dad's factory: as a signal for ordering widgets.

You: Yes, exactly. Now let's talk a little more about that. We already have crates implemented, and we can check their contents to see if they need to be replenished. But the widgets are being generated out of thin air. What models are we missing?

Student: Some sort of supply source? Because that's the whole point, right? We want to show that removing widgets from a crate triggers some other process that produces replacements automatically. So every crate should be associated with a supplier, and that supplier should be able to detect when the crate needs refilling.

Nasir: It sounds like you're suggesting that suppliers should be monitoring the status of the crates, which isn't entirely correct. Instead of the supplier checking to see whether a crate needs filling, a supplier should be notified when items are removed from a crate.

Student: How about an observer that gets called whenever pop( ) is called on a crate?

You: These are all interesting ideas, but we're getting ahead of ourselves. Let's limit our scope for now and think, "OK, we've already received a refill order. What objects need to collaborate in order to make that happen?"

Nasir: Good point. Figuring out how events should flow through the system is a separate concern from the actions that need to be carried out when an event occurs. Let's take this one step at a time.

As the students are starting to discover, one challenge of designing a system from the bottom up is untangling the connections between objects so that they can be implemented in small slices rather than big chunks. But this is an important skill to develop because it enables an incremental style of design.

* * *

You sketch out a rough workflow for resupplying a crate. In doing so, you introduce an Order object that will be responsible for associating a particular supplier with a particular crate:

One student asks what the point of the Order object is—wouldn't it be simpler to allow a Supplier to operate directly on a Crate?

This is a good question, especially at such an early stage in the project's development. It's true that every model you include in a design adds some conceptual baggage, so introducing superfluous objects into the mix is something worth avoiding.

But in this case, *not* modeling an Order object would lead to a potentially confusing merge of physical and logical system behaviors.

On a real factory floor, upstream suppliers directly load materials into crates, making it seem like the Crate is the relevant object that needs to be acted upon. However, the crates themselves are just containers that convey nothing more than a limit on the quantity of goods that might fit in them.

The real information about where the crate is going to be delivered to is either memorized by the workers on the line, printed out on a sheet of paper, or listed on a label that is attached to the crate itself. This is what the Order model represents. It's easy to miss because it isn't as visually obvious as materials being loaded in and out of a crate, but it is part of the domain model nonetheless.

With all the questions about the `Order` object wrapped up, you jump into implementing the resupply workflow. After a short while, the square and circle in your simulation are joined with a triangle and a line, and you're well on your way to teaching a basic geometry class:

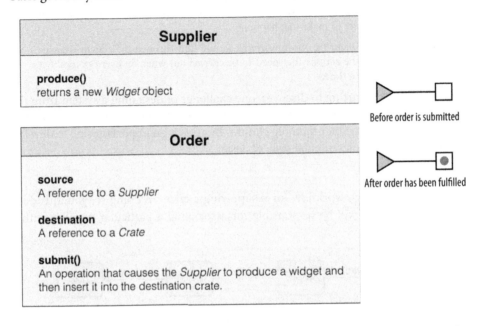

These simple shapes represent far more interesting stuff going on under the hood, so although they do not look like much they are still a meaningful sign of progress.

You explain to the students that when the space bar is pressed, the `order.submit()` method is called, causing a supplier to produce a widget. Once generated, the widget is pushed into the destination crate to complete the order. The students begin to see how these basic building blocks will soon be combined in ways that will give rise to a much more interesting simulation model.

Avoid unnecessary temporal coupling between objects

After a few days, it is time for your second demonstration. Since the last session, the only significant modification you've made to the simulator codebase is to enlarge the size of crates so that they can contain multiple widgets:

This small but important change allows your model to support the three essential quantities[1] in software design: zero, one, and many. Your earlier examples only dealt with the first two cases, but from here on out you need to work with all three.

With a mechanism for resupplying crates already built, your next step is to trigger a refill automatically whenever items are removed from a crate. You ask the students for suggestions on how to do this, and one suggests calling `order.submit()` immediately after any call to `crate.pop()`.

You make this small change and fire up the simulator. A full crate is displayed, and you inform the students that you've wired up the space bar to do as they suggested. You tap it once. Nothing happens. You tap it again—still nothing happens. Then you jam on the keys wildly, and the display flickers slightly, but for the most part, you're staring at the same full crate that you started with.

You put some logging code in a few places to confirm that keyboard input is being received, that both `crate.pop()` and `order.submit()` are being called, and that there aren't any unexpected loops or recursive calls. Everything looks fine. You comment out the `order.submit()` line and press space a few times and the widgets get removed one by one. You start with an empty crate and comment out the `crate.pop()` call instead, and the crate fills up one by one.

Nasir asks the class if they know what is going wrong, and one student quickly points out that the removal of a widget and the insertion of its replacement are happening in the same animation frame. Because there is no delay between the two actions, it appears as if nothing is happening.

To test this theory, you temporarily randomize the colors of the widgets being produced. Although this demonstration generates a massively disorienting effect, it proves the point quite well.

You: Now that we know what's wrong, how do we fix it?

Student: Make the `Supplier` sleep for a second before it generates a new widget?

You: That's a good idea, but we're working in an asynchronous programming environment. So there isn't a direct way to tell a process to sleep. Instead, you'd set up some sort of callback to be executed after a set period of delay.

Student: OK, do that then.

You: I would, but it's not so simple. Right now when `order.submit()` is called, it immediately triggers a call to `supplier.produce()`, which returns a `Widget`. The returned `Widget` is then pushed into the `Crate`. If we change `supplier.produce()` to use an asynchronous callback, it will no longer have a meaningful return value, breaking the whole chain.

---

1 This is called the *Zero-One-Infinity Rule* of software design, and was originated by Willem van der Poel.

Nasir: So what we have here is a classic case of *temporal coupling*. There is a timing dependency between the `Order`, `Supplier`, and `Crate` objects, because of the way they've been designed. We'll need to rework things to really solve the problem, but as a quick workaround, let's delay the entire order submission process so that it doesn't get executed until a second or so after the keyboard input has been received.

You implement Nasir's suggestion and try it out. Sure enough, a widget disappears from the crate as soon as you hit the space bar, and it is replenished about a second later. You then remove three widgets in rapid succession, emptying the crate. After a moment, the crate is full again, with all three replacements arriving at roughly the same time.

The students are happy to see that things are working, but you're quick to inform them that this is a bit of a hack. In order to make things work properly, the workflow will need some revisions.

You draw up a sequence diagram describing the new way that events will flow through the system whenever an order is submitted:

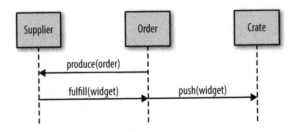

The changes needed to implement this revised workflow aren't huge.

First, you split up the responsibilities for the `Order` object so that submitting an order and fulfilling an order are modeled as two separate events. From there, you modify the `supplier.produce()` method to allow it to communicate via a callback rather than a return value.

With this new design, `order.submit()` still calls `supplier.produce()` immediately, but from there it is up to the `Supplier` object to decide if and when to call `order.ful fill()` and complete the transaction.

After Nasir asks the students a few questions to confirm their understanding of this minor refactoring, it becomes clear that they are able to trace the execution paths correctly, but they still don't quite understand the motivation behind the change.

You suspect that the problem is the students have not yet seen how this new workflow leads to a flexible timing model. You quickly implement three different variants of `supplier.produce()` to clarify that point:

1. *Synchronous*

   Directly call the `order.fulfill()` method. This causes widgets to be resupplied instantaneously, as they were in the original design.

2. *Asynchronous (concurrent)*

   Use an asynchronous timer to run the `fulfill()` method after one second, allowing orders to be processed simultaneously.

3. *Asynchronous (sequential)*

   Drop all incoming orders into a queue that is processed sequentially at a rate of one order per second.

Each of these implementations behaves very differently, but all three are supported using the same `Order` interface. This proves that the temporal coupling present in the original design has been eliminated, and that the system can now support whatever timing model you'd like.

The class briefly discusses the different possible timing models and their tradeoffs:

- A synchronous model would work well for a step-based simulation, where an event loop executes the actions one tick at a time. But this would mean either giving up real-time interactions with the system, or writing messy code to "fake it."

- An asynchronous concurrent model would be interesting, but without a more complex UI it'd be difficult to reason about simultaneous order processing.

- An asynchronous sequential model would strike a balance between the other available options, in that it would allow real-time interaction with the system as a whole by accepting new orders as they arrived. But the flow of widgets through the system would have a consistent, predictable rhythm to it.

You suggest that the asynchronous sequential model might provide the right balance between "interesting" and "easy to implement"—and the students agree with that decision. Had this been a real project with preset requirements, you may not have had the luxury to make this decision yourself, but breaking temporal coupling between objects would still have allowed the decision to be deferred until later.

Gradually extract reusable parts and protocols

So far, you've built suppliers and crates, and you've come up with an ordering mechanism for refilling crates on demand. These basic building blocks provide most of what is needed to run a just-in-time production simulator; from here, all that is left to build is a "machine" that serves as both a consumer and producer of widgets.

After talking through some ideas with the class, you decide the machine will be responsible for converting two input sources into a combined output stream. To get everyone thinking, you put together a mockup that shows what the simulator might look like once we add this new feature into the mix:

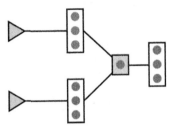

Nasir attempts to get the students to explain how to implement this new model, but they seem overwhelmed. When you take a moment to think about why, you realize the students are focusing on what makes this system different from what they've already seen, which has clouded their view of what has remained the same.

Taking a step back, you ask the students to consider a simplified system, made up entirely of parts they are already familiar with:

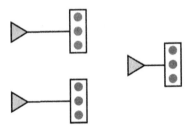

You: In this example, there are three suppliers and three crates. To make it easier to understand, assume these subsystems are completely independent from one another. What happens if we remove a widget from any one of the crates?

Student: That will trigger a resupply order to be submitted, and then after some time, the supplier will fulfill the order and a replacement widget will appear.

You: That's correct! Now let's make a tiny tweak to the system. Suppose that every time the supplier on the far right fulfills an order, it also consumes a widget from each of the crates to the left of it. What happens then?

Student: The crates on the left would need to be restocked, so orders would automatically be sent to their suppliers.

You: Exactly. Now if you revisit the mockup from earlier, it should be easier to understand how machines work. They'll produce output just like a supplier, but in the process of doing so, will consume widgets from upstream crates. When that happens, that will trigger resupply orders to their suppliers, creating a small but complete just-in-time production workflow.

After hearing your explanation, another student suggests making a Machine a subclass of a Supplier, in order to reuse the current Order object. Rather than responding to this suggestion directly, you invite the class to review the Supplier object's implementation and come to their own conclusions.

The students see that the core responsibility of the Supplier object is simple: it generates a new widget, and then calls order.fulfill() to complete a resupply transaction. This would be achievable with a single line of code if the Supplier immediately fulfilled its order, but the simulation's timing model complicates things a bit.

Buried in the internals of the Supplier object, there is a bunch of code that implements a rudimentary asynchronous sequential work queue. Nasir quickly points out an opportunity to reuse this code, because machines will need to implement delayed order processing in much the same way that suppliers already do. The only remaining question is *how* to reuse the code:

> **Student:** So is this a good reason to create a subclass? It looks like there is quite a bit of code that could be shared between the Machine and Supplier objects if we did.
>
> **Nasir:** Well, let's ignore everything else those two objects have in common for a moment, and think purely about this work queue implementation. It's just an ordered list of arbitrary functions that get executed one-by-one after a fixed time interval. What about this process is specific to the concept of a Supplier?
>
> **Student:** Nothing really, I guess. Are you saying it's just an implementation detail?
>
> **Nasir:** Not exactly. I'd say it's a missing abstraction in the toolchain we're using. An asynchronous work queue is an extremely generic construct, but since we don't have one baked into the language we're using, it was necessary to build one from scratch.
>
> **You:** I had thought about making the work queue its own object from the start, but then I realized it might lead to this fascinating conversation if I opted to defer that decision until later.
>
> **Nasir:** So in other words, you elected to make a just-in-time design decision? How very meta of you!

Despite the cheesy pun, deferred decision making is an important part of bottom-up design. Extracting objects too early and then trying to imagine future use cases can lead to awkward interfaces; but when you fit an interface to real needs, it is easier to come up with a better design.

Getting back to the problem at hand, you take a few moments to move some functions around in the codebase, and then produce the following API documentation for the newly created Worker object:

Worker
delay The amount of time to wait between jobs. **performAsync(job)** Adds a job to the work queue. **run()** Start an event loop that processes jobs one-by-one, at a fixed interval defined by the *delay* property.

After this refactoring, there isn't a whole lot of code left in the Supplier object, so the temptation to use it as a base class goes away. Instead, you copy and paste the few bits of useful boilerplate that remain and begin implementing the Machine object.

You start by adding some basic functionality for associating machines with upstream supply crates, which goes smoothly. But things get a little more complicated from there, and you need to make a few adjustments to the Crate object in order to support the new Machine construct.

The changes you end up making are not huge, but they represent the kind of warping and bending that can happen when an object gets reused outside of the context it was originally designed within:

- In the simple relationship between a single supplier and a single crate, it's not important to know if a crate is empty or not—as long as a resupply order is submitted whenever a widget is removed from a crate. But a machine can only fulfill its order when all of its upstream supply crates have widgets in them, so you implement crate.inStock() method to access this information.

- Every order holds a reference to a crate, but a crate does not hold a reference to an order. This works fine at the top level of the system where both Crate objects and their associated Order objects are defined, but it gets messy when you bring machines into the mix. To make it possible for a machine to both consume widgets from its input crates and submit a resupply order at the same time, you use a hack involving a closure that is neither elegant nor easy to explain.[2]

---

2 A proper fix to this problem would have been to go back and add a reference to a specific Order in the Crate object, but imagine that the visiting instructor was pressed for time and didn't want to think through that design decision yet. Instead, a workaround was cooked up on the spot that swept those details under the rug and allowed the lesson to focus on other, more important points.

You freely admit that unexpected design warts at the connection points between objects are one of the downsides of building things from the bottom up. But to restore a sense of optimism, you show the students a working version of the machine, complete with live updating counts of the orders flowing through the system:

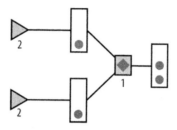

Despite the fact that you refactored some internals and added a few helper methods, no breaking API changes were needed to support this new feature. That is a sign that the overall design is working out well so far.

Experiment freely to discover hidden abstractions

Now that the hard work is done, Nasir gives the students some time to suggest small changes to the simulation that might test the strengths and weaknesses of its design.

They start with things you expected, like varying the speed of production and size of the crates for different suppliers and machines. It's fun to watch the system dynamically rebalance workloads in response to bottlenecks. They continue to explore these ideas for a while, but the outcomes do not reveal much of anything about the simulator's design.

To steer the students toward a slightly more interesting discussion, Nasir asks them to suggest a new kind of machine to implement. One student recommends modeling a purification process: a machine that operates on a single input source and produces a single output, but transforms the type of widget in the process.

Nasir starts to respond to the student, but before he can finish, you already have the new machine up and running. You feed its output into a combiner machine to make for a slightly more interesting example:

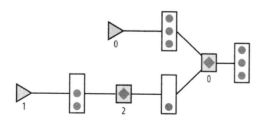

At first, Nasir assumes that you've already considered the possibility that a student would ask this question and wrote some code in advance to account for it, but you quickly reveal that isn't the case.

Instead, it has to do with how you've defined the concept of a combiner: it's a machine that consumes a widget from each of its input supply crates and then produces some output widget.

From this definition, it's possible to derive a purifier machine as a combiner with just a single input supply crate. And because of that, you are able to implement this new feature without writing any new code.

Another student takes things even farther down the rabbit hole by suggesting it might be possible to create a machine that works the same way that the Supplier object does by having no input supply crates, because an *all* condition applied to an empty set is always true.

This suggestion catches you by surprise, because you hadn't thought about that at all when you first built the supplier objects. But sure enough, it works!

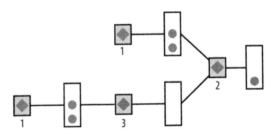

The students come up with other variations on this theme, including circular dependencies between machines, and multiple machines feeding from a single input source —all of which work as expected, even though you never explicitly planned for those use cases when building the system. The emergent properties of systems designed from the bottom up are fascinating, and are often difficult to predict.

Sensing the lesson has reached a good stopping point, Nasir attempts to wrap things up by telling the students that although this kind of experimentation is a lot of fun, it's only meant to help discover possible abstractions that could then be formally supported if they prove to be useful. It's not an invitation to discover a "hidden feature" and immediately put it into use without careful thought.

The students seem to understand this point well, and you're glad Nasir reminded them of it because sometimes you forget it yourself.

Know where the bottom-up approach breaks down

Feeling glad that the class ended on a high note, you start to pack up your things when a student asks if there's time for just one more question:

> **Student:** Can this technique of casually experimenting with a domain model also be used to identify the weak spots of a design?

> **You:** Absolutely. You can, of course, poke holes in anything if you look for weird enough edge cases; but if you stay within the realms of reason and run into problems, it may be a sign of a problem that needs to be addressed sooner rather than later.

> **Student:** Well, how about this? Machines can easily handle zero, one, or many inputs. But so far, we've only tested them with a single output. What if we build a splitter machine—that is, one that takes a single input source and then generates two outputs?

> **You:** Hmm…great question. I'd need to think on that one for a bit.

A few students linger after class as you spend a few minutes trying to add a splitter machine to the simulation. Eventually you get something working, but you're not happy with the way the code looks.

You start to think about why this feature was so much harder to implement than the others, and that's when you notice the fundamental difference in structure. The combiner, purifier, and generator machines all fit the pattern of n inputs being mapped to a single output (where n=many, n=1, and n=0, respectively). But the splitter would map n inputs to n outputs, and that changes the nature of the problem.

This is not necessarily a sign of a bad design, but it illustrates the tradeoffs between the top-down and bottom-up approaches. In a top-down design, you would have thought about the supported machine types at the beginning of the process, and then built an abstraction to support those cases. That might have led to a system that had more carefully thought out integration points, but it would have complicated the code for the simple cases—and would have required a more involved planning process.

You explain to the students that in practice, top-down design and bottom-up design work like a spiral. Bottom-up design is good for exploring new areas and keeps things simple as you get some software up and running. When you hit dead ends or rough patches, then top-down mode is useful for considering the bigger picture and how to unify the connections between things. The two techniques are not at odds with each other; they're just meant to be used for different purposes.

The student who asked about the splitter machine smiles as you thank her for asking an excellent question. Nasir jots down notes to share with the others who missed this bonus lesson, but you can tell that those who stuck around are glad they did.

Recommendations and reminders

- To get started on a bottom-up design, list a handful of important nouns and verbs in the problem space you are working in. Then look for the shortest meaningful sentence that you can construct from the words on that list. Use that sentence as the guiding theme for the first feature you implement.

- As you continue to add new functionality into your project, pay attention to the connections between objects. Favor designs that are flexible when it comes to both quantities and timing so that individual objects don't impose artificial constraints on their collaborators.

- When extracting reusable objects and functions, look for fundamental building blocks that are unlikely to change much over time, rather than looking for superficial ways to reduce duplication of boilerplate code.

- Take advantage of the emergent features that can arise when you reuse your basic building blocks to solve new problems. But watch out for excess complexity in the glue code between objects: messy integration points are a telltale sign that a bottom-up design style is being stretched beyond its comfort zone.

Questions and exercises

Q1: Some work environments are well suited for a bottom-up design style, while others aren't. What are some non-technical (i.e., business level) obstacles that could get in the way of applying the techniques discussed in this chapter?

Q2: Suppose you've decided to build your own email client. What are the important nouns and verbs in this problem space? What is a simple sentence using those words that might describe a good starting point for a first feature to implement?

E1: Spend 20–30 minutes studying the concept of Connascence (*http://connas cence.io/*), and write down some notes on how it relates to the ideas from this chapter.

E2: Answer Q2 and follow through with implementing the minimal slice of functionality you identified as good first feature for an email client. Narrow the scope as much as you can to complete this exercise in a single sitting.

CHAPTER 6

Data Modeling in an Imperfect World

Imagine that you work for a small business that is in the early stages of replacing a decade-old time tracking application.

Your coworker Mateo was the main developer for the original application, which replaced a tedious paper process that everyone hated. The software has served its purpose over the years, but a decade of constant use has revealed some of its weak spots. In particular, the application's core data model has a few rough edges that should not be carried over into the new system.

Because you weren't involved in developing the original application, Mateo is counting on you to look at the project with a fresh pair of eyes. You've spent the last few days reading the old codebase and playing around with ideas, and today you'll present your plan for building a better system.

The challenge will be to balance what is technically ideal with the needs and working style of the company. Data modeling and workflow design go hand in hand; they work best when they're thought about together.

Mateo will help you with the historical context around the project, and the two of you will work together to design a replacement that can serve the business for many years.

In this chapter...

You will learn how small adjustments to the basic building blocks of a data model can fundamentally change how people interact with a system for the better.

Decouple conceptual modeling from physical modeling

You begin with an idealized example of how employees use the time tracking system on any given workday:

- 8:30 AM: Clock in at the start of the workday.
- 1:30 PM: Clock out when leaving for lunch.
- 2:30 PM: Clock in after returning from lunch.
- 5:15 PM: Clock out at the end of the workday.

In the current application, this sequence of events would create a pair of WorkSession records, which are modeled as intervals in the database. One would run from 8:30 AM to 1:30 PM, and another from 2:30 PM to 5:15 PM.

You point out that this design makes sense as a conceptual model, but it unnecessarily complicates raw data manipulation. Mateo asks you to give an example and you're happy to do so:

> **You:** Suppose an employee forgets to clock in at 8:30 AM, but remembers all the rest of their punches for the day. What intervals will be created then?
>
> **Mateo:** Hmm…it'll misinterpret the 1:30 PM punch as an IN punch, because that would be the first punch entered for the employee on that day. From there, it'll create an interval from 1:30 PM to 2:30 PM, and then another that starts at 5:15 PM but leaves its finish time undefined.
>
> **You:** Exactly! Until this error gets corrected, the data itself will be out of sync with reality, in a pretty confusing way. To make things worse, editing the data to get things back into a consistent state would involve touching four separate fields spread across two records, which is a confusing process.

You illustrate your point by showing a table with the two work session records and how they would need to change:

IN	OUT	WORKED
~~1:30 PM~~	~~2:30 PM~~	~~1.00 HRS~~
8:30 AM	1:30 PM	5.00 HRS
~~1:30 PM~~	~~NULL~~	~~NULL~~
2:30 PM	5:15 PM	2.75 HRS

You also mention that you've taken a look at how often missed punches happen in the system, and that the data shows that this is a daily headache for the management staff.

Mateo spends a moment thinking about the problem, and he remembers that it is a relatively recent one. Up until a couple of years ago, employees only punched a clock twice a day. In that original workflow, the employee would have punched in at 8:30 AM and out at 5:15 PM, then a predefined amount of lunch time would automatically be deducted from their hours. With only a single IN punch and OUT punch per day, times could be edited as needed without any complications.

Seven years after the system was created, company policy changed and it became mandatory to record punch times for all breaks. The system needed to be updated to support this new rule, but it was done on a shoestring budget, and by then the code-base had degraded in the way that legacy projects left untouched for years often do. Under those constraints, the idea of improving the workflow to fit the new requirements was out of the question.

You've identified this design flaw as a problem that is worth fixing in the new system, and have a specific solution in mind:

> **You:** My goal is to eliminate the need to modify a good punch in order to correct an error. If you need to add a missing punch, it should be possible to key in that one missed time while leaving everything else untouched.
>
> In order to make this happen, we'd stop modeling work sessions as intervals in the database, and instead record punches as individual events. From there, we'd convert raw punch data into intervals at the application level whenever we need to display a report or run a computation.
>
> **Mateo:** This won't change the fact that if a punch is missed, the timesheet will still show incorrect IN/OUT pairs until it gets corrected.
>
> **You:** That's true, although in the current system it isn't just the reports that can break—the data itself gets corrupted. So you end up editing a bunch of fields just because the system put the punch data in the wrong place.
>
> With the new model, basic facts of the system stay accurate even if the reporting still gets out of sync with reality in certain edge cases. Whenever an employee records a punch, that actually happened, so the system can treat it as a fact. Work sessions generated from those punches are a muddier concept, and this approach cleanly separates the two.
>
> **Mateo:** Got it! Then yeah, this makes sense. I still would like to see an example of how the new model will work, though.

You draft up another quick figure to demonstrate that in the new model, a missing punch can be directly added to the punch list with no other modifications needed:

Punches
8:30 AM
1:30 PM
2:30 PM
5:15 PM

From here, you can convert the data into `WorkSession` objects at the application level by creating a new interval for each consecutive pair of punches. But since these intervals would be dynamically generated at runtime, no special consideration needs to be given to them when the raw punch data is updated.

In a system with messy data sources, it's often better to preserve some degree of flexibility by not imposing too much structure at the physical data modeling level.

Design an explicit model for tracking data changes

There's only so much you can guess at when staring at code that was written a decade ago, so you ask Mateo to fill in some details about how the existing system handles audit logging. He shares a bit of the backstory with you to help you understand what needs drove the implementation of the feature in the first place:

- It was well understood from day one that the software needed a comprehensive audit trail for any changes to time records. The data in this application corresponds directly to what employees get paid—meaning the potential for fraudulent management activity couldn't be ignored.

- Original punch data from employees would also need to be reviewed from time to time, to catch discrepancies in employee records. For example, if someone consistently misses punches or requests that later punch times be adjusted to reflect an earlier start time, it could be a sign of a problem.[1]

- The auditing requirements were understood to be protections against truly exceptional circumstances. In the entire history of the application, the company has only needed to dig into these logs a handful of times—so history has proven that assumption to be accurate.

---

[1] In the best-case scenario, this might mean figuring out what is causing the employee to begin working before clocking in. But in the worst-case scenario, this pattern of behavior could be a sign of someone intentionally falsifying their time records. In either case, an audit log is helpful for detecting the problem and can also serve as evidence later as to why the behavior is being questioned in the first place.

To keep costs down, Mateo used a third-party library that provides functionality similar to that of a backup mechanism, but for database records. So whenever a record in the old system is updated, the workflow looks something like this:

1. Create a read-only copy of the record before it is modified.
2. Update the record with whatever changes you need to make.
3. Update the admin_id field to indicate who approved the change.
4. Increment the record's version number.

The copied records are stored in their own versions table, but have all the necessary information to review changes between versions, or revert to an old version if necessary. The main caveat is that because this is all done at the database level, the concept of a revision is tied to a record insert or update, rather than to a meaningful business transaction.

To demonstrate how the versioning mechanism would work for the *"add a missed punch at 8:30 AM"* scenario you've been using throughout the discussion, Mateo cooks up the following example:

Work Session Versions

Punches

8:30 AM
1:30 PM
2:30 PM
5:15 PM

SESSION_ID	IN	OUT	ADMIN_ID	VERSION
1001	1:30 PM	NULL	NULL	1
1001	1:30 PM	2:30 PM	NULL	2
1001	8:30 AM	1:30 PM	1234	3
—	—	—	—	—
1002	5:15 PM	NULL	NULL	1
1002	2:30 PM	5:15 PM	1234	2

He attempts to explain how this works, knowing that it's a confusing process that ought to be improved upon in the new system:

Mateo: In order to add the missed punch, a new version gets created for each of the two work sessions. And you can see from the data that these changes were made by a manager, because they include an ADMIN_ID.

You: But how do you show that these two changed records are actually part of a single change request?

Mateo: You can't. Not directly from the data, anyway. You'd have to pull the full history of work sessions for an employee on a particular day and just infer what happened from the changes that were made.

You: So, you mean like noticing that the 2:30 PM OUT time in version 2 of session 1001 ends up becoming the IN time in version 2 of session 1002?

Mateo: Uh…yeah. This is super confusing, and the few times I've needed to run reports against it, I scratched my head for a while until I sorted out what happened; then I'd send a clean report to the management team. The data itself is a giant mess, though. I'm thankful that the need to work with it has been so rare that I haven't had to think about this much.

You: I imagine it easily gets even worse, too. What happens if there's a typo when the manager enters a revised time, and then they go back and correct it later? Does that create a new version too, even if they fix it immediately after submitting the change?

Mateo confirms your point with a nod, then tells you that he recognizes the weak spots. He is very interested in hearing your new path forward.

You start describing a design where the audit log isn't a bolt-on feature implemented at the database level, but instead is explicitly modeled as part of the business domain.

Knowing that some sample data will help Mateo understand better, you then show him the following example:

Timesheet Revisions

Punches

| 8:30 AM |
| 1:30 PM |
| 2:30 PM |
| 5:15 PM |

WORKDAY	NOTE	ADMIN_ID	ID
2016-03-17	Missed first punch of the day	1234	1001

Punch Adjustments

ACTION	PUNCH_TIME	REVISION_ID
add	8:30 AM	1001

You explain that a `TimesheetRevision` represents the high-level information about a change: which workday it is for, a note explaining why the change is needed, a reference to the admin who approved the change, and so on. From there, the `PunchAdjustment` model captures the individual punch that needs to be added to the timesheet.

You then show Mateo a few examples of how your new model would support some of the other change requests that are common within the company.

An employee who forgets to punch in until after an early morning meeting:

Timesheet Revisions

Punches

WORKDAY	NOTE	ADMIN_ID	ID
2016-03-17	Arrived on time but punched in late	1234	1001

Punches
8:30 AM
9:17 AM
1:30 PM
2:30 PM
5:15 PM

Punch Adjustments

ACTION	PUNCH_TIME	REVISION_ID
add	8:30 AM	1001
remove	9:17 AM	1001

An employee who forgets to record their lunchtime punches:

Timesheet Revisions

WORKDAY	NOTE	ADMIN_ID	ID
2016-03-17	Forgot to record punches for lunch	1234	1001

Punches
8:30 AM
1:30 PM
2:30 PM
5:15 PM

Punch Adjustments

ACTION	PUNCH_TIME	REVISION_ID
add	1:30 PM	1001
add	2:30 PM	1001

These examples illustrate some of the benefits of the new design, but Mateo still has a few questions for you:

Mateo: Overall, I agree that this approach makes the audit trail easier to understand. But what else does this do for us?

You: Honestly, I modeled things this way at first just to clean up the auditing system, but then I realized that it can enable a much better workflow for administrators.

Mateo: How so? I can't really see that from what you've shown so far.

You: In the existing system, WorkSession records are edited directly, and the auditing tool you are using creates a read-only backup before any modifications are applied.

But when you edit multiple WorkSession records simultaneously as part of a single change, there's no easy way to tie them together. This limits (or at least complicates) the kinds of features we can implement that would make the punch editing process less error prone.

Mateo: Can you be more specific? Keep in mind that I probably have serious tunnel vision because I've been thinking in terms of how the old system has worked for over a decade now.

You: Sure! Wouldn't it be nice if you could review the pending changes to a timesheet before updating the official records?

If we use the `TimesheetRevision` model to generate a live preview, any mistakes could be corrected before the changes were committed and signed off on.

Mateo: Hmm…yes! That would be useful. Now I think I get why you modeled things this way: you're planning to use the `TimesheetRevision` and `PunchAdjustment` models to drive changes to the `Punch` records, rather than the other way around.

You: Exactly. I'm attempting a rough approximation of the *event sourcing*[2] pattern. By representing the changes we'd like to make to the timesheet as a sequence of `Punch Adjustment` events, we can defer updates to the raw `Punch` data until later.

Still trying to wrap his head around the event sourcing pattern, Mateo asks what would happen if the data ended up in an inconsistent state. But the whole point of modeling things this way is to avoid that problem in the first place.

The event sourcing pattern models individual events as immutable data; they're raw facts and they never change. By running through a sequence of events and computing a result, you can get a projection of the current state of the system. But since data flows in one direction in an event-based model, that state will always be exactly equal to the combination of events that generated it.

For each individual `Punch`, the complete lifecycle is straightforward. Punches can only be created in one of two ways: via the timeclock that employees use to clock in and out, or via a `PunchAdjustment` that is approved by a manager.

No matter how it is created, once a `Punch` record comes into existence, its timestamp never changes. The only change that can happen to a created `Punch` record is for it to be marked as removed, and the only way that can happen is through an approved `PunchAdjustment`. Once a `Punch` is removed, it is never interacted with again.

You point out to Mateo that in this sense, a `Punch` in the new system only has two states: created and removed. And since each `TimesheetRevision` represents a coherent batch of changes to punches, you can make sense of what was modified and why.[3]

Mateo pauses to think for a moment before asking a follow-up question:

Mateo: This idea sounds promising, but how will we deal with conflicting `Timesheet Revision` requests? It could get confusing if you have two requests simultaneously: one to add a punch and another to remove a punch, and they get approved separately from each other.

---

2 Event Sourcing (*http://pbpbook.com/event*) is a pattern that is meant to make changes to a data set explicit, reversible, and auditable.

3 This problem is well suited for event sourcing because of its small number of possible state transitions. More complicated models might require complex database queries, and might have performance concerns that you would need to consider when evaluating the tradeoffs of different modeling patterns.

You: That's a good question. If many different batches of changes to a timesheet were open simultaneously, that would get pretty confusing, and could lead to inconsistent data. And we certainly don't want to think about doing N-way merges!

To prevent these complications, we can constrain the system so that no more than one `TimesheetRevision` can be in an open state for each employee/workday combination at any point in time. An open `TimesheetRevision` can have adjustments added to or removed from it before it is approved, but the combined result will be a single coherent timesheet for the day in a "pending" state.

Mateo: OK. We'll need to see how that works in practice, but it seems like an acceptable constraint for now.

As this discussion wraps up, you notice that there is a common theme that seems to be guiding your new design: reducing incidental complexity as much as possible by minimizing mutable state.

There is a whole lot more that can be said about this topic,[4] but you're already itching to move on to your next big idea.

Understand how Conway's Law influences data management practices

Organizations which design systems are constrained to produce designs which are copies of the communication structures of these organizations.
—Melvin Conway

You ask Mateo how timesheet change requests are currently handled by the business, and he comes to realize that may be the biggest weak spot in the current workflow.

The process is completely ad hoc; each employee who needs a change communicates it to their manager by whatever method happens to be convenient for them: whether it's an in-person conversation, an email, or a phone call. The manager then reviews and aggregates these requests before sending them along to the payroll administrator, who makes the changes within the time management system.

The feedback cycle is variable, but it's often on the slow side. Confirmation of a change can take days, and there tends to be a rush around the end of the pay period to get all the timesheets reconciled so that checks can be cut. If a request gets dropped or some details about it get miscommunicated, it might take several passes through the feedback loop to get corrected.

---

4 For a very interesting read on how mutable state can greatly increase the complexity of a program, see Ben Moseley's "Out of the Tar Pit" (*http://pbpbook.com/tarpit*).

Employees have discovered a workaround for this broken process: if they submit their requests directly to the payroll administrator through an internal messaging feature within the time tracking system, they tend to get acted on quickly, and with greater accuracy. But in doing this, they cut their own managers out of the loop, which is suboptimal from an administrative perspective. Some employees file duplicate requests in an attempt to both follow the rules and get a quick response, which results in even more confusion.

The company is big enough where this messy process creates friction daily, but small enough where fixing it hasn't been a high priority. But it's clear that an improvement would be welcome as long as it wasn't too costly to implement. Your theory is that this problem will be easy to solve in the new time tracking system, because the new data model will open up doors that were previously closed.

> **You:** I know this might be a hard sell, but I think the real way to fix this issue is to let employees adjust their timesheets themselves.

> **Mateo:** I was afraid you might say that. I think it's a great idea, but this is a really tough topic to get into with management. I don't even know where to begin the discussion on this, because it is such a departure from how things are typically done around here.

> **You:** Well, what do you think the major stumbling blocks are? What are they likely to be most concerned about?

> **Mateo:** For starters, I think they'll be worried about technical training issues. Part of the reason why the payroll administrator keys in all the changes rather than having the managers at each office take care of that is because early attempts to train management staff on the timesheet editing process didn't go well.

> **You:** Not to be too harsh, but do you think the poor design of the original system had anything to do with that? Editing four text fields just because you want to add a single punch to a sheet seems awkward even for a programmer.

> The old system also had no way to review your changes, no way to easily undo a change, and no way to edit a whole day's worth of times at once. You were brought to a separate form for each time interval you edited—a consequence of using an auto-generated admin panel rather than building a custom interface.

> **Mateo:** So you're saying my user-hostile interface is to blame? I'm not sure I would have agreed a decade ago, but I've definitely changed my perspective since then. But it's also such a large timescale that expectations around human-centric design have really shifted, even in business applications.

> That said, there are still plenty of programs in use here that were built 20 years ago or more, all of which are even more awkward to use than the time tracking system. All of this contributes to a generally uneasy relationship with software throughout the company, and so even if we can convince them that we can build something learnable, we'll need to go beyond that to get their approval.

> **You:** Well, what else do they really care about? If we know what matters to them, we can find a way to emphasize those points when suggesting a change to the workflow.

Mateo: I know the management staff cares a great deal about accuracy, even though they take a very messy approach toward obtaining it. The idea of overpaying or underpaying an employee because their timesheet wasn't correct is especially bothersome to them, and rightfully so.

Their theory is if the payroll manager keys in all the changes, that leaves a single person directly responsible for maintaining accurate records. That one well-trained person knows all the common mistakes staff members might make, and can follow up when a request looks problematic.

You: What do you think? Does that approach really work as well as they think it does?

Mateo: I think given the limitations of the existing system, they have an effective process in place. The main problem is that this creates a huge amount of work for one person, and it's unclear to me whether that's a cost effective way of doing things or not.

You: OK, I think I have a way to deal with these concerns. Before I get into that, what else do you think matters here?

Mateo: Well, the other major recurring theme is a strong desire for effective oversight. Even minor discrepancies tend to be followed up on, as a proactive measure to limit fraud and abuse.

The tradeoff is that active monitoring tends to erode trust within the company, and it also eats up time that managers might be able to spend on more important issues.

As you think through the cultural values that influence how the company operates, you begin to see which design constraints are most important to keep in mind.

You realize that for an improved timesheet editing workflow to even be considered, the proposed alternative would need to be easy to use, and it would need to make data entry errors easy to catch and correct. It would also need to preserve or even extend the effectiveness of management oversight built into the current process.

You believe that your planned workflow will meet all of these needs—and then some. Mateo seems somewhat skeptical, but is also excited to hear your suggestions.

Remember that workflow design and data modeling go hand in hand

Mateo agrees that allowing employees to modify their own timesheets could be a major process improvement, as long as you frame it in the right way.

To make things more concrete, you point out several specific benefits that would come along with switching to this new way of doing things:

- As long as employees are able to preview the changes they make to their timesheet before submitting them, they will know exactly what to expect if and when their request has been approved. This will help prevent data entry errors due to miscommunications about what changes are needed.

- Assuming that all pending changes are clearly marked, timesheets and other reports can be immediately updated to reflect the requested changes rather than continuing to display incomplete or inaccurate information.

- Instead of relying on managers who are spread across half a dozen offices to aggregate requests and forward them to the payroll manager, all of the requests will be directly entered into the system by employees and the only step that will remain is to review and approve the changes. This will cut down on a huge amount of error-prone busy work for the management staff.

- If there is an open question about a particular change, all of the management staff as well as the employee who submitted a change request will be looking at the same information at the same time. If a request needs to be modified, then that too will be updated in real time and visible to everyone who needs to see it.

- Because this new change request system would move official requests to modify timesheet data into the time tracking application itself, the paper trail would be far more complete and consistent than what is currently in place at the company.

- Notifications about accepted and declined changes could be automated, preventing the possibility of a decision being made without it being communicated.

- Warnings could be presented to the payroll manager whenever there are still pending timesheet editing requests at the end of a pay period.

All of these potential benefits hinge on having an implementation that works well enough to overcome the friction of change. You've done a few technical spikes around these ideas and sketched up some mockups; now it is time to share what you've come up with.

At the heart of your solution is a presenter object that combines two key pieces of data: the punches that have already been committed for a particular workday, and the proposed adjustments to that list of punches.

This combined data set will be used to present three important pieces of information: what the timesheet looked like before a requested change, what it will look like after the change is applied, and a summary view of exactly what the changes are.

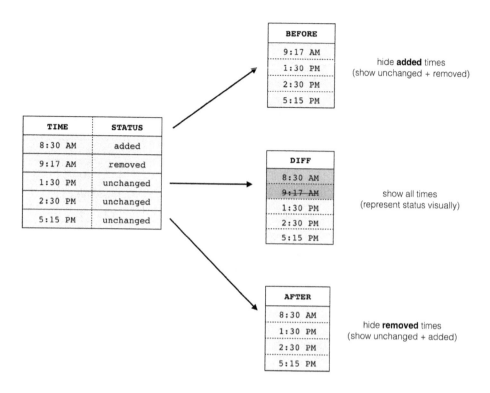

You point out that the AFTER view of data isn't just meant to be used to preview the final state of a request; it can also be updated live as individual PunchAdjustments are added to a TimesheetRevision. This makes it possible to mimic direct punch editing in the user interface:

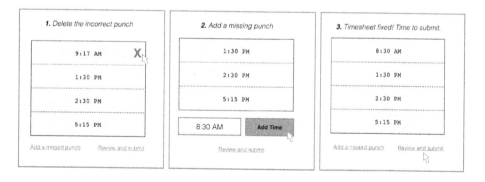

When the employee is ready to submit their request, they are shown the before, after, and diff views side by side. After reviewing their changes to make sure they are accurate, they fill in a notes field explaining why the change is needed.

Once the request is submitted, it appears alongside all other open requests in the management panel, looking something like this:

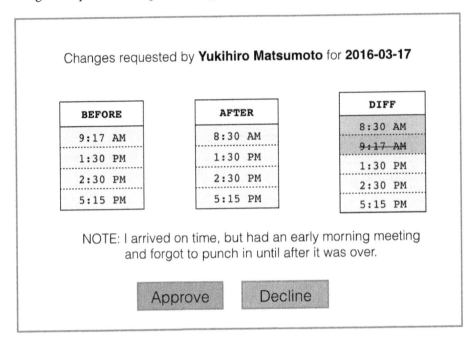

If the request is approved, then a new `Punch` for 8:30 AM will be created, and the 9:17 AM `Punch` will be flagged as removed. If it is denied, then the `TimesheetRevision` will be closed without any `Punch` data being modified. In either case, the timesheet will return to a state in which there are no pending changes.

The critical feature of this workflow is that official time records used for computing employee paychecks are only ever modified when the payroll manager approves a change. This achieves the same centralized control and oversight that is baked into the current process, but streamlines the communication around a change in a way that should greatly reduce data entry errors.

As you look back on your suggested improvements to the core data model, it becomes immediately apparent that each minor revision set the stage for the next improvement. What strikes you about the new design is that it doesn't make massive, earth-shattering changes to the original model; it only requires relatively small tweaks to the way that data is stored and interacted with in the system.

There is no guarantee that this new workflow will be accepted by the business; the practical constraints of politics and budget always need to be considered. That said, you're confident that at least some of these ideas will survive in the new system and make things better for all of the people using it.

Recommendations and reminders

- Preserve data in its raw form, rather than attempting to transform it immediately into structures that closely map to domain-specific concepts. You can always process raw data into whatever form you'd like, but extracting that same information from complex models can be needlessly complicated.

- As you develop a data model, think through the many different ways the data will be presented, queried, and modified over time. Very few real projects are limited to straightforward create, read, update, and delete operations on individual records…so plan accordingly.

- Make it easy to preview, annotate, approve, audit, and revert transactional data changes in a human-friendly way. Implementing this type of workflow involves writing custom code rather than relying on pre-built libraries, but applying the event sourcing pattern in your data models can simplify things a bit.

- Design data management workflows that respect and support the organizational culture of the people using your software. Systems that do not take Conway's Law into account tend to be crushed under the weight of a thousand workarounds.

Questions and exercises

Q1: The time tracking workflow described in this chapter is a good fit for a business with a few dozen employees spread across a handful of offices. What would a system designed for a five-person, single-location business look like? How about a 5,000 person business with 50 locations?

Q2: Does the software used by and produced by your workplace match its culture and communication style? If not, what consequences are there for the cultural mismatch between the business and its software?

E1: Pick any software you have worked on recently and think about how its data could reasonably become out of sync with reality due to human error. Investigate how these failure scenarios are currently handled in your application, taking notes on whatever bright spots and dark corners you find.

E2: Use the event sourcing pattern to model a simple Tic-Tac-Toe game with the following features: save, restore, undo, and move-by-move game replay. If you want to take things a little further, also add branching points in the game transcripts.

CHAPTER 7

Gradual Process Improvement as an Antidote for Overcommitment

Imagine that you are a consultant that specializes in helping early-stage product companies overcome their growing pains.

Your newest client is a few months into a transition from a web development agency to a product-based business. Their core focus is on a product called TagSail, a mobile-friendly web application that helps people find nearby yard sales.

The business model for TagSail is straightforward: the site is free to use for anyone looking for yard sales to visit, but a fee is charged to anyone who posts a listing on the site. There are also premium features available to paying customers, but like many early-stage products, TagSail's offering is a bit scattershot.

For months it looked like the product wasn't going anywhere, but in recent weeks it has started to gain traction. This spike in activity has caused major strains at both the technical and human level, and the team is now at the point where they're willing to try anything to prevent themselves from being swept out to sea.

Your mission is to help the TagSail team minimize waste while still delivering a steady stream of value to their customers. To make this happen, you'll apply Lean-inspired process improvements—but custom-fit to the needs of the situation on the ground.

In this chapter...

You will learn some common anti-patterns that lead to struggles in software project management, and how incremental process improvements at all levels can alleviate some of those pains.

Respond to unexpected failures with swiftness and safety

It's your first day on site and there is already a minor emergency underway. A reverse geocoding API is failing, causing all requests for TagSail's home page to fail with a generic internal server error.

You ask Erica (the company's lead developer) to fill you in on the details:

> **You:** I know that this isn't the time for a long conversation, but can you take just a minute to get me up to speed on what's happening here?
>
> **Erica:** Sure. We had a huge traffic spike this morning because our site was mentioned in some popular newsletter, and that caused a major slowdown in page load times. We increased the number of server instances to try to keep up with demand, which helped for a little while. But then a few minutes ago our reverse geocoding service started rejecting all requests, completely breaking our home page.
>
> **You:** So as of right now, no one is able to use the application at all?
>
> **Erica:** That's correct. They'll see a generic "We're sorry, something went wrong" message that gets served up whenever an internal server error happens. That's pretty terrible, because this is by far the most visitors we've ever seen in a day.
>
> **You:** Any idea how much longer it will take to get the site back up and running again?
>
> **Erica:** I'm not sure yet. We're still trying to figure out exactly what went wrong with the reverse geocoding API, and how to get it working again. We think it's probably some sort of rate limiting issue.

You continue to observe for a few minutes, and suggest that the team might be focusing on the wrong question. Rather than looking into fixing the broken API, they should focus on getting the home page up and running again—even if it means degrading functionality slightly.

After a brief discussion, the developers come to realize the reverse geocoding is not essential, anyway. A separate set of APIs detect the visitor's geographical coordinates and center the map on their location; the reverse geocoding service is only needed to turn those coordinates into a meaningful place name that gets shown in the search box above the map.

Temporarily disabling the reverse geocoding API calls would leave the location search box blank. This could cause a minor usability headache in situations where the detected location was inaccurate, because the first thing the visitor would see would be a map centered on a specific location that wasn't their own. But even in that scenario, the visitor could still manually enter their location into the search box, and everything would work as expected from there.

Although most of the team seems comfortable with this idea, Sam (the team's most experienced frontend developer) pushes back a bit. He suggests the root cause of the problem could be properly fixed by moving the server-side reverse geocoding API calls to the client side, eliminating the rate limiting issues and also fully restoring site functionality. You briefly discuss the tradeoffs with Sam and Erica:

> **You:** Have you already built the client-side implementation, or are you planning on writing the code for that right now?

> **Sam:** Well, when we first built this feature I'd suggested doing it that way, and I did a quick spike to prove the concept. I'm not sure if I still have that code laying around, but the documentation was easy enough to follow.

> **You:** How long do you think it'd take you to make that change, if we went that route?

> **Sam:** It'd be a quick fix, I think. Half an hour of work at the most.

> **You:** When you did your proof of concept, how realistic of an environment did you test the work in? Did you simulate lots of simultaneous requests? Did you try it in all the browsers that the product needs to support? Did you actually expose it to live production traffic?

> **Sam:** Um, no. But this API is provided by FancyMappingService. I'd assume that it's pretty solid given how common of a use case this is, and how popular their service is.

> **You:** You know what, I think you're probably right. But I also worry that experimentation under pressure tends to go poorly. If we disable the feature that'll take the pressure off, and allow everyone to think more clearly.

> **Erica:** How about a compromise? Sam can begin working on a patch that will move the reverse geocoding to the client side, and I'll buy us some time by disabling the feature for now. That should only take a few minutes, and in the worst case I can revert and we'd be back to where we are now.

> **You:** That sounds fine, as long as you wait until after the system has returned to a stable state to begin experimenting with Sam's patch.

Erica gets to work on disabling the reverse geocoding feature, which goes smoothly. She asks you whether or not it'd be a good idea to deploy her fix right away, but you point out that even in chaotic situations like this, it is better to ask for a quick review than to rush work out the door that might make a bad situation worse.

Erica opens a pull request for Sam to review before the two of you take a quick walk around the office just to see how everyone else is holding up.

After waiting for what feels like too long, Sam finally sends Erica an update via chat; he's still working on his own patch, which he thinks will be ready to ship in another 15–20 minutes. He also wants to skip the temporary workaround and go straight to deploying his own fix.

You don't say anything, but the look on your face makes it clear that you're not happy with this response. You walk across the hall to Sam's office and close the door.

Five minutes later, Erica receives a notification that her branch has been deployed. Immediately after that, you return to her workspace with Sam in tow. Erica pulls up the server logs and the three of you monitor the system together.

As the request logs tick away on the screen, they clearly show that people are successfully loading the home page again. There is a big spike in the number of manual lookups of locations, as expected.

Convinced the site is stable again, Erica asks Sam to resume work on the client-side patch. With the immediate pressure relieved, there is no rush to get that fix out the door—so it can be properly reviewed and tested before it is rolled out.

Identify and analyze operational bottlenecks

It's been a week since your last visit, and the first thing you ask Erica is what new features have shipped in the last few days.

When she tells you, "Nothing, unless you count bug fixes," it is impossible to miss the faint look of disappointment in her eyes. You waste no time and get straight to work:

> **You:** So if no new improvements have been rolled out in the last week, what has each person on your team been up to?
>
> **Erica:** Let's see...I've started to integrate a few new classified ad networks with our application.
>
> Sam has been working on a new version of an internal library we've built, in preparation for some new features we plan to implement next month.
>
> And finally, Sangeeta and David started on an improvement that we planned to ship this week, but then there were some urgent support requests that needed attention. They had to put their feature work on pause in order to take care of those issues.
>
> **You:** What were the urgent support requests?
>
> **Erica:** They were also related to our classified ad integrations. A few weeks ago we added support for an ad network that is pretty popular, and it seemed to work well at first. But it turns out that the new version of their API only supports certain regions, and for other regions you need to use their old API.
>
> The differences between the two APIs are small enough that we thought we could share a common client between them as long as we didn't use any newer features, but that turned out to be a mistaken assumption.
>
> **You:** So how did you find out about this problem?
>
> **Erica:** Through bug reports from users. We don't have a very good monitoring mechanism in place for the integrations at this point, so we rely on our support team to be our eyes and ears.
>
> When something comes up only once or twice, we assume it's an isolated issue and then review and prioritize the bug reports weekly. When three or more reports show up for the same issue, it gets escalated and someone looks into it immediately. That's what happened in this case, and it ate up the second half of David and Sangeeta's week.

You: But the issue they investigated is sorted out now?

Erica: Well, we *think* so. We don't have direct access to several of the systems we integrate with, and in particular, don't have staging environments set up for every possible version of every system we support. Their fixes seem to have sorted out the issue for the people who filed the bug reports, but it's a little hard to tell if we've managed to fully fix the compatibility issues or not.

You: This sounds like kind of a nightmare, in general.

Erica: It is! I think we spend at least half of our time in a given week on these integrations, and I have my doubts that they'll ever pay off enough to be worth the time we're putting into them.

You ask Erica how requests for new integrations are being processed, and she shows you a tiny form on the customer dashboard that says, "Don't see your local classified ad provider? Let us know and we'll try to support it soon!"

Erica explains that this form generates many requests, but the team is struggling to fulfill them because the effort to integrate each service is highly variable. Sometimes there are web-based APIs that are easy to work with, and other times an "integration" can be made up of an ad hoc email report, a spreadsheet uploaded to an ancient FTP server, or even a text document delivered to a fax machine.

The word *fragile* does not even begin to describe TagSail's classified ad network support, but the sales team is (somehow?) convinced that taking on that pain so customers don't have to will pay off in the end. Suspecting that there is something not quite right here, you start to dig a bit deeper.

Pay attention to the economic tradeoffs of your work

For many phenomena, 20% of invested input is responsible for 80% of the results obtained.
  —Pareto Principle

You spend a few minutes reviewing the project's issue tracker. It turns out that new requests for integrations are flowing in five times faster than the existing requests are being closed. When you add in bug reports, the ratio is actually closer to 8:1.

These are bad numbers because it means most requests sit indefinitely in limbo and the backlog keeps growing and growing. Left unchecked, this will become an even greater maintenance headache than it already is.

There is a clear process problem with how classified ad integrations are being handled, but its relative severity depends on how much the work is (or isn't) paying off for the company. You ask a few more questions to get a more complete picture:

You: What is the business model for ad network integrations?

Erica: We bill the customer for whatever the external costs of running the ad are, in addition to the base cost for listing their yard sale on our own website.

You: So in other words, these integrations don't provide direct revenue themselves; they are just one of the benefits offered to customers?

Erica: That's correct. And honestly, we didn't originally plan to roll this out nationwide. We initially integrated with a single major provider in New England. We were hoping that might get us some publicity and attract new paying customers, and it managed to do both. But we didn't have much of a plan for where to take things next, and the requests started flowing in.

You: Then let me guess: the sales team got excited by the early results and made a push toward supporting as many integrations as possible?

Erica: Yep, and without really talking with us about it. The first integration was built in a single day and was able to serve dozens of cities; it didn't occur to them that future integrations may take a lot longer than that to serve a much smaller market.

You: I think I'm beginning to see the problem here.

With Erica's help, you do a tiny bit of market research. You dig up a statistical report,[1] which claims that the average number of yard sales in the United States per week is around 165,000 and that the leading online classified site posts around 95,000 listings per week for the whole country.

Erica runs a quick query against TagSail's data to find that they're posting roughly 15,000 listings per week, which is just shy of 10% of the nationwide average.

Of the customers posting those listings, about half of them have access to at least one classified integration. In that group, about one in eight opt into paying the extra fees associated with getting their ads listed in their local newspaper and online news sites. That breaks down to an average of roughly 1,000 total listings per week that make use of the classified integrations feature.

You then ask Erica to break down the average number of listings per integration. From the raw data she comes up with, you produce the following graph:

---

1 In case you are curious, here is the real statistical report (*http://pbpbook.com/stats*) that forms the backdrop for this made-up story.

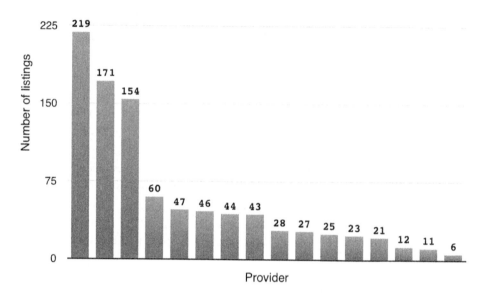

Average number of listings per week by provider

The story makes sense in hindsight, but it's an uncomfortable thing to think about: almost three in five classified ads are handled by the top three integrations, and the bottom 50% of the integrations handle only a little more than 15% of the listings. With relatively few customers using the integrations to begin with, supporting these less popular services is effectively a total waste of time for the development team.

You encourage Erica to report these findings to Jen, the head of the product team. She hesitates, doubting that her concerns will be considered because they go against a priority of the sales team. But when you point out that neither the product team nor the sales team has access to the data that was used to generate this new report, Erica warms up to the idea that she might be taken seriously this time around.

Jen and Erica get together to discuss the problem while you listen in and act as a moderator. Once there is some basic agreement that a huge portion of the integrations work is mostly going to waste, you lay out some concrete suggestions on how to bring things back into balance:

- Focus support efforts on the eight most popular integrations, which cover 83.6% of all listings per week on average.

- Set a fixed limit on capacity (say 20% to start with) that can be allocated to work on integrations each month. If the team goes over this limit, report back to the product team so they can revise their plans accordingly.

- Audit the eight less popular integrations and decide what level of support to offer for them, if any. Those that are working with very low maintenance overhead could possibly be kept around, but the high-cost integrations could be gradually phased out.

- Work with the product team to evaluate potential market sizes and cost of implementing and maintaining integrations before adding more ad networks. Make sure that it's clear that any time spent on integrations is time not spent on other potentially valuable work.

- Make it clear to customers that there is no guarantee that new classified ad providers will be supported, and consider removing the request form entirely.

- As the integrations workload stabilizes, invest in proactive maintenance measures like better monitoring, logging, analytics, and testing. Prioritize work on these preventative measures based on experienced pain points rather than theoretical future needs.

The purpose of this plan is to put an upper limit on the amount of effort that can be invested in developing an area of the application that's producing diminishing returns. Although often overlooked, simple time budgeting is a powerful tool for limiting the impact of the high-risk areas of a project, and also encourages more careful prioritization and cost-benefit analysis.

If even some of these changes materialize, life should get a whole lot easier for the development team while also freeing up a large amount of time to focus on more productive work.

Reduce waste by limiting work in progress

Four weeks pass, and then you join the TagSail team again to see how things are going. Your first question is whether or not they've managed to get the issues around classified ad integrations under control, and Erica is happy to report that they seem to have gotten that area of the product to finally settle down.

You then ask what new improvements they've shipped since your last visit, and Erica lamentingly tells you: not much, unless you count bug fixes, chores, and internal code cleanup. You pull yourself together after a moment of uncomfortable silence and start to dig in:

You: I don't understand. Didn't you free up about 30% of the team's capacity and also radically reduce unplanned urgent work since the last time we talked?

Erica: Yes, but as soon as the product team saw that we were no longer putting out fires every day, they began to pile on new work to make use of our newfound capacity.

They seem obsessed with the idea of "catching up" with the roadmap we created before we ran into growing pains, and that has us back in a tough spot again.

You: So what's happening? Is work being rushed out the door before it's ready just to make room for the next set of tasks?

Erica: Nope, that's not it. What's happening is new work is being planned and assigned every week, but the product team is very slow to respond to our questions and sign off on finished work so we can ship it. We're also running behind on our own internal code reviews and QA testing, because the whole team is opening pull requests much faster than we can close them.

You: Believe it or not, this is a sign of progress. Removing one bottleneck in a process will naturally cause another one to become visible,[2] and it seems like the new constraint is how fast work can be reviewed and approved before it is released. Finding the right cadence and sticking to it will take some effort, but once that's taken care of, you should start to see some real forward momentum.

Erica: If you mean asking the product team to reduce the amount of new work they assign per week, that's going to be a non-starter. They have commitments to uphold the hectic schedule they'd put in place when we were trying to go for a new funding round, and so there is a ton of pressure all around to deliver new work quickly.

You: But work that is stuck in code review isn't delivered yet, and neither is work that sits around in a queue for days or weeks waiting to be approved by a product manager before it can be shipped. You can have a hundred improvements in a work-in-progress state, but the only thing generating value is the stuff that ships.

Erica: I agree, but how can we get the product team to change their approach?

You: It's simple if not easy: we need them to establish the mindset that unshipped code is not an asset, it's inventory. Moreover, it's perishable inventory with a cost of carry.

Erica had explained this problem to the product team before, but she approached it from a different angle. She emphasized the harmful costs of context switching, and the stressful feeling of starting new things before finishing existing tasks.

You point out that while those are completely valid concerns, it's better to frame the conversation in terms of the negative impact on the team's ability to deliver new valuable work to customers. To find evidence to support this point, you ask Erica to show you the team's Kanban board:

---

2 For more on this concept, research Eli Goldratt's Theory of Constraints (*http://pbpbook.com/goldratt*).

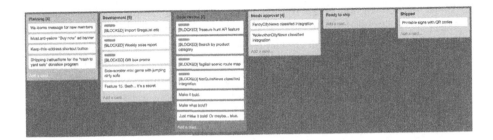

Almost immediately, you notice the right side (which represents deliverable and delivered work) is nearly empty, while the left and center sections (which represent planned work and work in progress) are richly populated. There are also many blocked tasks, which—if unblocked all at once—would cause severe overload.

To solve this problem, you will need to talk to Jen, who is responsible for deciding what gets worked on each week. Erica gets her on the phone and listens in as you try to talk through the critical disconnect between the planning rate and delivery rate on the project:

You: A few weeks ago we made some changes that I hoped would have sped up progress, but from what Erica tells me things still aren't moving all that smoothly. How does it look from your perspective?

Jen: Good in some ways and bad in others. A good thing is that the developers seem to be less overwhelmed with urgent bug fixes lately, so they're focused on productive work now. But there is still a ton of pressure from the CEO and our investors to rapidly grow the product, and many of our partnerships are hanging in the balance right now.

You: The main problem for the development team is that new work is being piled on before they have a chance to ship or even finish their current tasks, and from what I can tell, they seem to be making a reasonable complaint.

The last significant customer-facing improvement was completed six weeks ago, and currently there are two new features waiting to be signed off on. But there are twelve features in a work-in-progress state, and four more are being planned!

Jen: I know, it's a big mess. What can we do about it?

You: Well, how many new pieces of functionality can you realistically release per week?

Jen: Our original roadmap called for one major improvement along with 2–3 minor improvements per week. The plan was to send out an email newsletter every Tuesday to announce the changes and show people how to use them.

You: That seems reasonable on paper, but new work is being planned much faster than it is getting shipped. As a result, you're accumulating work in progress, and much of it is blocked on feedback. The overall flow rate is what matters, and when you have much more flowing into the system than out of it, that's how things get overloaded.

Jen: I see what you're getting at. Part of the problem is that we're expected to keep the developers busy. That means that whenever there's an open slot on the Kanban board, it's a signal to us to sit down with a developer and plan a new feature. Now that they're moving a little bit faster, this is actually taking up a fair amount of our time.

You: Why not use that time to help unblock the developers who have questions or need approval? Wouldn't that help make sure they stay productive and also lead to more work getting shipped, sooner?

Jen: If I could make those decisions on my own, I absolutely would. But few questions the developers ask are ones that I can answer directly; some require conversations with the sales team, others involve customer research, others require talking to vendors and partners, and for some I even need to sit down with the CEO and talk them through.

Unfortunately, sometimes a question that only takes ten minutes for the right person to answer can take a week or more to get a response.

You: OK, I understand the problem now. You're trying to stick to a development pace that is faster than your feedback bottleneck.

This never works, so we either need to slow down the release cadence, reduce the batch sizes of the work being done, or speed up the feedback loops. I'd recommend some combination of all three for best results.[3]

There is some initial resistance to the idea, but after a lengthy meeting with the CEO, you and Jen come out with a plan that seems almost too good to be true:

- Put a hold on planning new major features for four weeks to allow some of the current work in progress to be wrapped up and delivered.

- Change to a release cycle of one new major feature every two weeks, with the first new release planned for four weeks from now.

- Release minor improvements on a rolling basis, rather than allowing them to block or be blocked by the newsletter announcements.

- Gradually build up a backlog of up to five release-ready features to serve as a buffer for when a current major work in progress is blocked.

- Once that buffer is built up, synchronize planning with the release schedule so that a newly released (or canceled) feature is what triggers the planning of a new major improvement, rather than trying to max out available developer capacity.

- Review the product roadmap and cut it in half. Involve both the sales team and the developers in this process to know the costs and benefits of the revised plan.

- Block off four hours company-wide on Monday mornings for coordination time. During this time, no one will be expected to do heads-down work or attend formal meetings; instead, the entire time period will be used for helping anyone who is blocked get unblocked.

---

3 Donald Reinertsen's *The Principles of Product Development Flow* (Celeritas Publishing, 2009) is an excellent (if abstract) read on this topic.

The overall goal is to give the entire organization a bit of room to breathe. By letting backed-up work make its way out the door before cramming in just one more thing, a more natural and stable rhythm of work will hopefully emerge.

That said, this plan is just a starting point, and you make it clear that Jen and Erica can expect it to be challenging at times to keep the whole company committed to it. For that reason, you've suggested running it as a twelve-week experiment to start with, and seeing how things go from there.

Make the whole greater than the sum of its parts

Three months go by like a flash. As you predicted, it hasn't been easy for everyone to stick to the plan, and there have been times where some team members have been tempted to go back to their old way of doing things. But they've reluctantly stayed on course, and some of your ideas have definitely paid off.

To help you get a sense of how things went over the last twelve weeks, the CEO requested that each department come up with "a rose, a bud, and a thorn" to sum up the last few months of work.

The roses represents good things that have happened, the buds reflects things that look promising, and the thorns are pain points:

	Rose	Bud	Thorn
Sales (Steve)	All five major features released in the last 12 weeks have shipped on schedule.	Continuous delivery of minor improvements may boost the reputation of our product.	Our current growth rate is still falling far short of original projections.
Support (Lena)	The average defect rate for new feature has gone down dramatically.	Customers are starting to notice how quickly we're able to respond to urgent issues.	Many minor problems and "nice to have" feature requests are being rejected because they aren't on the short list of priorities.
Product (Jen)	Fewer concurrent tasks in a WIP state has allowed designers to focus on quality rather than quantity.	As we build up our buffer of release-ready features, we'll have more flexibility to decide what gets released, and when.	Sales team is still emphasizing novelty factor when planning new work, rather than focusing on improving what we already have.
Development (Erica)	Work is rarely blocked on feedback now, and the impact is minimal when it is.	Leaving enough time in the schedule will help us incrementally pay down tech debt.	We feel left out of the product design process, which is making coding work harder than it should be.

This may be the first time the organization has created a high-level view of how decisions affect everyone as a whole in spite of frequently holding inter-departmental meetings in the past. The fact that they're doing this exercise at all is a sign of better collaboration within the company, even if there are many problems still left to be resolved.

The four department leads begin an uneasy conversation about each other's thorns, but it soon begins to feel like they're talking past each other. You calmly suggest that they take a short break before continuing the discussion.

When they return, you ask each person to write down a brief explanation of "why it hurts" for each of their pain points. You then present all of their responses side by side, so that they can see their own concerns in the context of the bigger picture:

	What hurts	Why it hurts
Sales (Steve)	Our current growth rate is still falling far short of original projections.	Without a 50% increase in top line revenue over the next six months, we will start to hit major financial problems and need to either seek another investment round or downsize.
Support (Lena)	Many minor problems and "nice to have" feature requests are being rejected because they aren't on the short list of priorities.	Most minor issues are tolerated but still negatively impact customers. Left unchecked for too long, these problems can cause death by a thousand paper cuts.
Product (Jen)	Sales team is still emphasizing novelty factor when planning new work, rather than improving what we already have.	The current approach of adding everything under the sun to the product makes for an impressive feature list, but is leading to an incoherent product design.
Development (Erica)	We feel left out of the product design process, which is making coding work harder than it should be.	When the product team prioritizes and plans work for us without asking us to review it for technical feasibility, they're attempting to guess at the value of a feature without knowing its cost.

The discussion picks back up again, but this time around you volunteer to moderate things to make sure that the group stays focused:

> **You:** I'd like to start with Steve's concern, because it's the elephant in the room. The product is making money, but it's not cashflow positive—let alone profitable. With over 20 people on staff here, that's a scary problem and one that needs to be on the top of everyone's minds.
>
> **Jen:** This is the first time I've seen Steve explain this in terms of runway rather than projected revenue growth. I think everyone in the company is able to understand the former, whereas the latter seems abstract.
>
> **Erica:** I don't know, I'm not sure how the developers on my team would be if I told them, "In six months some of you may be out of work if we can't turn this thing around at a breakneck pace."

Lena: I agree, and I'm sure that people from the support team would be first to go, should we need to downsize. This is terrible news.

Steve: Unfortunately, the sales team isn't responsible for defining a reasonable growth rate; we're tasked with trying to hit the numbers that the CEO and the company's investors have laid out for us. We're staffed for a growth curve that's much steeper than our actual results can justify, and it's been that way for a few months now.

You: But doesn't that mean that the product roadmap is also tracking based on an assumed growth curve that just isn't there? In other words, are we applying a "go big or go home" strategy when we don't have the resources to pull that off?

Steve: Well, I guess you can say that. The reason is because 50% growth over six months is just the bare minimum we'd need to keep extending our runway rather than shrinking it. To make our investors happy, we'd need to hit something like 150% revenue growth over the next 180 days.

You: Let's assume for the sake of argument that there's no reasonable way to get within striking distance of that goal. If you cut those projections in half, would it allow you to shift the focus to selling what is already built for a while rather than gambling on new major features?

Steve: We'd need to get approval from the CEO, but it may be worth trying for a couple months. But we'd also need to prove that the approach is working with hard numbers.

You point out to all the non-sales people in the room that in a business that's not profitable yet, cash is oxygen—things go bad quickly when it runs out. It's not a pleasant thing to think about, but forgetting it is how you go out of business.

At the same time, the financial success of the product is directly tied to how well the staff as a whole can work together. Building a better, more cohesive product means balancing the needs of everyone involved in its development, without emphasizing the needs of one team over the others.

Taking into account everything that was revealed in the "roses, buds, and thorns" exercise, you help the group come up with a plan that will help them stay aligned with one another as they go through the next few months of critical work on the product:

- Build a new dashboard that lays out the core AARRR metrics (Acquisition, Activation, Retention, Revenue, Referral) that are essential to any business (*http://pbpbook.com/aarrr*). Having everyone look at the same reports, and training the entire staff on how to read them, will make it easier to get a sense of overall product health at a glimpse.

- Figure out where the AARRR pipeline bottleneck is and then have all teams work together to try out experiments that might help move the needle in that area. Start with incremental improvements, and gradually work up to more substantial changes as needed.

- Do an all-hands meeting to review the product onboarding process, both for visitors looking for yard sales, and customers posting listings. Have each employee take notes on any areas that can be improved.

- Look to see if any issues noticed during the onboarding walkthrough overlap with existing support tickets or items on the product roadmap. Prioritize those for fixing in the near future, and then use the AARRR metrics to measure impact.

- Set aside one day per week for a single developer to work on "small stuff" that the support team feels is worth fixing. Rotate this position each week so that all developers can get some experience with responding to support issues.

- Schedule time for as much cross-training as possible. Developers and product designers should sit in on sales calls, sales people should attend some project planning meetings, and everyone in the company should spend at least an hour per month doing front-line customer support.

- Identify three features within the next eight weeks that can either be removed from the product or significantly simplified. Specifically target the features that appear out of place in the context of the product as a whole.

The common thread that ties each of these individual actions together is a simple piece of advice: know enough about what everyone else is doing to be able to see how your own actions fit into the bigger picture.

After discussing this plan, the group expresses a fair amount of optimism about the coming months. There's no guarantee of success, but with a common understanding of the problems at hand, they're far more aligned than they were just days ago.

With a dramatic tone you say, "My work here is done," and then ride off into the sunset. As for everyone else, their work has just begun.

Recommendations and reminders

- When dealing with system-wide outages, disable or degrade features as needed to get your software back to a usable state as quickly as possible. Proper repairs to the broken parts can come later, once the immediate pressure has been relieved.

- Look for areas where you are overcommitted and constrain them with reasonable budgets, so that you can free up time to spend on other work. Don't rely solely on intuition for these decisions; use "back of the napkin" calculations to consider the economics of things as well.

- Remember that unshipped code is not an asset; it's perishable inventory with a cost of carry. Help everyone involved in your projects understand this by focusing on what valuable work gets shipped in a given time period, rather than trying to make sure each person on the team stays busy.

- When collaborating with someone who works in a different role than your own, try to communicate in ways they can relate to. Take an outside view, and think, "What about this issue is relevant to the person I'm talking to? How does it fit into the bigger picture of the project?"

Questions and exercises

Q1: Think of a rose, a bud, and a thorn from your current development process. Would other developers on your team have come up with similar ideas or different ones? How about the non-technical people involved in your projects?

Q2: Consider the metrics you are using to measure the overall health of your projects. Do they tell an accurate and meaningful story? If not, why not? If so, will they still be relevant six months from now, or will you need to measure different things by then?

E1: Choose one project that you're currently maintaining. Introduce a breaking failure into one of its features, and deploy it to a testing environment. Without "fixing" the broken feature, find a way to restore as much system functionality as possible by working around or hiding the problem with no more than 15 minutes of work.

E2: Keep a work journal for four weeks, listing out your main activities each day. Pick the three projects or recurring tasks that you suspect had the greatest payoff for the time invested. What sets these particular activities apart from the others in your journal? Is there a way you can scale your successes?

CHAPTER 8

The Future of Software Development

Just as in the previous chapters, you'll find a short story in the pages that follow. But since this chapter also serves as the book's epilogue, I'd like to step out of my narrator role for a moment to talk about something important.

I wrote this book because I believe the shift away from "programmer as coding specialist" is inevitable. If that's true, then our entire field will need to prepare itself for the not-so-distant future when "programmer as technically skilled solver of ordinary human problems" becomes the norm.

I've been writing code for a couple decades now, so this idea feels radical—and also quite liberating. The interesting parts of programming to me have always been the problem-solving, communication, and human-centric aspects of things; code was just the most effective tool I could find to serve those purposes.

The stories in this book have been written without code samples, but they have the explicit goal of helping both you and me focus on the many interesting higher-level challenges we face in software development. But in each scenario, there was a whole lot of code being written behind the scenes; it just wasn't what we were focusing on.

To complete our journey, we'll now go a step further and imagine a world in which machines do most of the coding. I promise to tie this back to some practical ideas when we wrap up, but we might as well have some fun before the curtain closes.

In this chapter...

You will catch a glimpse of what programming might be like if we could focus purely on problem solving and communication rather than writing code.

Imagine that you are in the center of a room that is nearly empty. It has been your office for the last five years, but it still reminds you of old science fiction movies every time you walk into it.

To make use of this workspace, you only need to wear a special set of goggles and gloves; the many sensors, cameras, speakers, and other electronic components that are buried in the walls take care of everything else.

Through your goggles, the room presents itself as a lovely corner office in a high-rise building with a perfect city view. That serves as a nice backdrop, but what really matters is the work you've come here to do.

You call out to your virtual assistant (Robo) and let it know that you're ready to start your day. It immediately springs into action, and helpfully reminds you of what you're supposed to be working on:

> **Robo:** Hi there! Carol from FutureTown's Department of Transportation has asked you to prepare a report that will help her set the budget for sidewalk repairs for the rest of the year. Should I load my notes on that project so that we can get started?
>
> **You:** Yes. We'll begin with some of the public data available about city service requests. Please show me the service codes table from FutureTown's 311 API.
>
> **Robo:** This table is a simple set of key/value pairs. Take a look at the center window in front of you if you'd like to review the whole thing, or let me know the specific key you are looking for and I will highlight it for you.
>
> **You:** I'm looking for sidewalks.
>
> **Robo:** I found a match for "Sidewalks and Curb Damage" with a value of 117.
>
> **You:** Yes. That's the one!

You reach out in front of you and pinch the air, right about where the "Sidewalks and Curb Damage" table row has been projected through your goggles. As you do this, it turns into small sticky note, which you place in your (virtual) pocket. You then swat at the large data table displayed front and center, and it vanishes instantly.

You ask Robo to show you a summary of all of the data sources provided by FutureTown's 311 service, and it fills the left wall of your office with documentation. You grab the sheet describing the "reported issues" table, and then sit down to think.

You're building this report because FutureTown is trying to figure out how much money to spend on sidewalk repair, and where in the city to spend it. As a starting point, some measure of supply and demand would probably help—which is why you're looking at the public 311 data.[1]

---

1 Despite the futuristic framing of this chapter, open city government data is readily available today. In fact, the examples in this chapter are based on SeeClickFix data (*http://dev.seeclickfix.com*).

You don't know exactly what you are looking for yet, but you decide to start with a few visualizations and see how that goes.

You: Robo, let's start by doing some work with this "reported issues" table. I have the data sheet in my hand, and you can use that for your queries.

Robo: Alright. What would you like me to do with this data source?

You: It has open and closed timestamp fields. Please use those to create a cumulative flow graph for the last five years, broken down by week. I'd like this visualized as both a figure and a data table, please.

Robo: All set! Please check the display and tell me if it looks right.

You: Whoops, I missed something! Robo, please only show records where the "service code" field matches the number on this sticky note.

Robo: Beep-boop-beep! Done.

You take a look at the numeric table just as a sanity check, and it looks roughly like what you'd expect. Then you look at the graph:

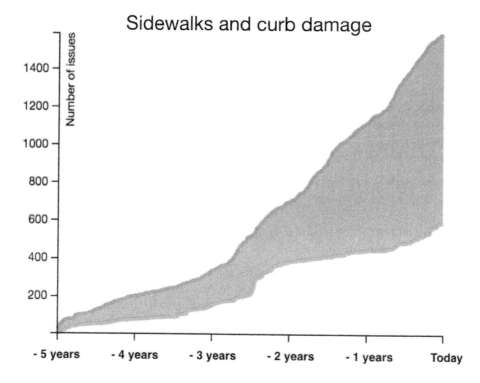

The huge spike in new complaints from citizens in the last few years makes it easy to see why coming up with a budget is so challenging for FutureTown: they don't have nearly enough resources to fully solve the problem, so they need to try to spend what they do have as wisely as they can.

You ask Robo to dump its research files, and in an instant the right wall of your office lights up with dozens of pages. They include a combination of materials you had looked up yourself the last time you did work for FutureTown, documents that Carol had shared with Robo when she first requested work on this project, and additional resources that Robo found itself using its internal recommendations engine:

> **You:** Thanks for the literal wall of text Robo. Please give me a one-paragraph summary of what I'm looking at.

> **Robo:** FutureTown's annual sidewalk budget is broken down by neighborhood. Neighborhoods with a high number of requests for repairs to sidewalks that have a pavement condition index (PCI) ranging from 20 to 60 on a scale of 100 are given the highest priority in budgeting. Below a PCI of 20, the cost of repair is prohibitively expensive for the current operating budget. Above 60, the sidewalks are considered to be serviceable enough to defer repairs.

> **You:** Thank you. Please highlight any document that mentions the pavement condition index, as well as any documents that mention neighborhoods.

> **Robo:** BEEEEEEEP. Done.

As smart as Robo seems at times, its research features are equivalent to that of a powerful search engine combined with a decently organized knowledge base. The thinking part is still left to humans, so this is where the real work begins.

You spend a few minutes looking over the highlighted documents, trying to get some inspiration. One of them is a detailed assessment of pavement conditions at hundreds of locations around the city, carried out last year by the city's engineering department. You snatch it up like the low-hanging fruit that it is, and toss it in the general direction of your main working space, where it snaps cleanly to the wall.

When you ask whether the project's research files include geospatial data for Future-Town's neighborhoods, Robo responds sharply that no match was found. But when you restate your question to ask whether there is geospatial data about FutureTown's neighborhood boundaries available on the Internet, the first match is the set of shape files you were hoping to find.

The data in the engineering report consists of street addresses and the PCI values for the sidewalk at each address. You ask Robo to first convert the street addresses into geographical coordinates, and then use those coordinates to match against the shape files for FutureTown's neighborhoods. This generates a new data table with the neighborhood name appended to each row.

Once this table is generated, you run some statistics that rank each neighborhood based on the proportion of samples in the 20–60 PCI range. This part of the equation will probably need to be checked and tweaked by city officials, but you provide this as a starting point for them to work with.

Finally, you go back to the cumulative flow graph you generated earlier and give Robo some instructions on how to group the reported issues by neighborhood as well. Not wanting to repeat yourself verbally, you switch to visual scripting mode, copy the relevant chunk of logic for mapping street addresses to neighborhoods, and apply the same transformation to the location field on reported sidewalk issues.

After applying some finishing touches, you end up with historical graphs of supply and demand for sidewalk repairs, broken down by neighborhood, sorted by their pavement condition rankings. You place the top six on the main wall of your workspace, and hang the rest off to the sides.

You send a notification to Carol that the report is ready for review, and within minutes, she is (virtually) standing alongside you, seeing the same thing you see:

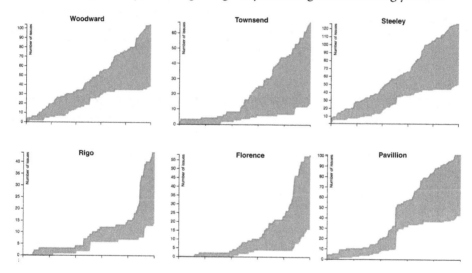

You briefly explain the logic behind your reports, while she walks around and pinches a few of the graphs to zoom in on different timescales. As the two of you chat, Robo records a video of your meeting and automatically transcribes the text of your conversation for future reference.

Carol: This is a very helpful starting point. I think the next step will be to look at these neighborhoods that are highly ranked, and dig in at the city block level.

Sidewalk equipment is costly to move, so the closer together the repairs are, the cheaper it is for us to do more of them. The ideal scenario is when you have a bunch on one street, because then the equipment doesn't need to be transported at all.

You: Alright, I can put something together for that. I assume that someone from the engineering department can give me some hard numbers on how to weight things based on how close together the jobs are?

Carol: I think so; I'll have them forward some documents over to Robo. Also, just this morning I was talking with a friend over in BiggerFutureCity and they said that they'd be willing to pass along their research files, as long as we agreed to share our own in the future. You may want to look through those and see whether there are any useful resources that we can use for our own reports.

You: Will do. Is there anything else I can help you with?

Carol: Oh, I hate to bring this up, but how many hours have you billed for this report so far? The city is pretty cost-conscious.

You: A little over an hour. I expect that if I do the block-by-block analysis and maybe dig through those other research files, we'll be done by midday and the total cost will come to about three hours.

Carol: That's perfect, thank you!

Carol disappears into thin air. Moments after she exits, your virtual workspace also dissolves, and you're left wherever you happen to be...with a programming book in front of you, and an author with a strange sense of humor saying his own goodbyes.

* * *

The story you just read describes my dream of what programming could be like once we finally claw our way out of the Turing tarpits.

The fictional workflow I've described in this chapter is just one possible human-computer interface that could satisfy my real goal: to communicate with computers at a high enough level to stay in problem-solving mode rather than being dragged down into thinking about the nuances of code.

Throughout this book, I've discussed many ways to work around the limitations of our tools, but I fully admit that the suggestions I've provided only partially relieve the friction we deal with day to day. In order for our industry to reach its full potential, we will need a development toolchain that is designed from the ground up to support human-centric values.

There are a handful of bright spots to take inspiration from that already exist today, albeit in specific problem domains. The humble spreadsheet is perhaps the best example the world has seen so far, and it's the source of inspiration for the interactions in this story:

- In a spreadsheet, if you want to sum up a column of numbers, it takes a only a couple of clicks and keystrokes. You think the thought, "I want to sum up these values," you visually select them, type the word SUM, and the sum appears where you typed the word.

- If you want a time series graph, you select a column of timestamps and a column of corresponding values, and then you click a picture of something that looks like a time series graph.

- If you want to share your work with someone else, you send along your file or give them access to a shared document—and they see what you see.

There is no separation between the data of a spreadsheet and the functions processing the data, no distinction between source code and a running program—it's just a document, but a very powerful kind of document that does what you tell it to do, without an awkward mental translation layer to some lower-level language.

Developer tools in modern web browsers have a similar feel to them, in that they let you directly interact with the page you're on, seamlessly blending the concept of a "document" with its underlying object model.

To find an <h1> tag in a document and tweak its styling is not a complicated task for anyone with basic HTML skills, but the time and context lost in doing so makes it feel like coding. By contrast, clicking on a header directly in the web browser, and then getting dropped right into an inline editor that lets you inspect the properties of the element and tweak it live has a totally different feel to it. It lets you have the thought, "I want to increase the font size of this header," and then work at that level rather than simulating the DOM in your head as you edit a static text file.

So how do we apply a similar mode of interaction to the sidewalk reporting problem I described in the main story for this chapter? The short answer is that we can't—at least not with our current development tools. But the good news is that there aren't any hard technical limits standing in our way, just the collective inertia of using processes and tools that weren't designed for modern application development.

* * *

As a thought experiment, let's quickly revisit the sidewalks report described earlier, setting aside all the virtual reality and artificial intelligence bells and whistles. Here are just a few totally generic operations involved in running that sort of analysis:

- Geocoding street addresses to geographic coordinates.
- Matching a geographic coordinate to a region that contains it.
- Exporting data tables from web services.
- Generating a cumulative flow graph from a data table.
- Running basic numeric aggregations (rankings, sums, averages, etc.)

In theory, a decent toolkit would make each of these operations something that could be done effortlessly, much in the way that we might put together a spreadsheet or tweak styles with a browser's development tools. In practice, it is much more complicated than that.

Because I've built reports quite like what was described in the story, I can tell you that there are many tools out there that can help with each of these tasks, and even in cases where you decide to build the tools yourself, you don't need to move mountains to get the job done.

But is it a fluid and natural process to use our existing tooling to run this sort of report? Absolutely not! It's a tedious exercise in pipe fitting between this third-party library and that language's core functions, this data format and that web service's protocol. The final product ends up being tied together with shoestrings and glue, unless you want to dig down into the code and "do things right," which comes at a high cost for questionable value.

And because of all of this incidental complexity, any real implementation of this simple report would involve asking the question: "Wait, what problem am I trying to solve again?" over and over as you struggled to keep the context fresh in your mind.

* * *

Although the field of software development has a long way to go, I do expect things will get better in the years to come. It's true that some folks among us are here solely for the tools, the code, the intellectual challenge of it all. But for the rest of us, that's a matter of necessity and the environment we work in, not a defining characteristic of who we are.

My fundamental belief is that programmers are no less concerned for human interests than anyone else in the world; it's just hard to make that your main focus in life when you spend a good portion of your day chasing down a missing semicolon, reading source code for an undocumented library, or staring at a binary dump of some text that you suspect has been corrupted by a botched Unicode conversion.

And my great hope is that if we fight against the influence of our rough, low-level, tedious tools and gradually replace them with things that make us feel closer to the outcome of our work, then our tech-centric industry focus will shift sharply and permanently to a human-centric outlook.

To put this into perspective, take any modern challenge and roll it backward to a time when code was written in assembly language and data was stored in manually packed binary blobs. In this sea of numbers and logical constraints, it is easy to treat the whole of software development like a pure math problem.

Such an abstract space is not a natural environment for empathy to arise from, so you could hardly fault someone who would unquestioningly fulfill their duties, particularly if they found their work to be intellectually rewarding for its own sake.

Now wonder: what will the next generation of programmers who come after us see when they look back at our times?

Take the actions today that will give you the reputation tomorrow that you'll be proud to have. For each of us, this will be different. But it is essential to consider the question, and there is much that we can do to help each other along the way.

For my part, I wrote this book. I hope that you've enjoyed it, and that it has given you some ideas that you can carry along with you throughout the rest of your journey.

Thanks for reading, and good luck with your work!

PS: If you have a question about this book or anything else you'd like to discuss, feel free to email me (*gregory@practicingdeveloper.com*), or tweet *@practicingdev*.

Well done! You just finished Programming Beyond Practices.

As a parting gift, please enjoy this final challenge.[2]

$	20	:	A	$	25	:	B	>	0B	>	37	50	52	4F	47
52	41	4D	4D	49	4E	47	20	42	45	59	4F	4E	44	20	50
52	41	43	54	49	43	45	53	50	52	4F	47	52	41	4D	4D
:	X	$	A	:	Y	^	>	35	49	4E	47	20	42	45	59
4F	4E	44	20	50	52	41	43	54	49	43	45	53	50	52	4F
47	52	41	?	Y	AA	+	X	-	Y	>	35	4D	4D	35	49
4E	47	20	42	45	59	4F	4E	44	20	50	52	41	43	54	49
43	45	53	?	B	F9	-	B	>	03	50	52	4F	47	52	41
35	4D	4D	35	49	4E	47	20	42	4F	4E	44	20	50	52	41
35	4D	4D	35	49	4E	47	20	42	4F	4E	44	20	4F	4E	!
35	4D	4D	35	49	4E	47	20	42	4F	#	X	^	>	37	41
$	0E	$	48	$	53	$	49	$	46	$	00	$	45	$	48
$	54	$	00	$	4C	$	4C	$	41	$	00	$	52	$	4F
$	46	$	00	$	53	$	4B	$	4E	$	41	$	48	$	54
$	00	$	44	$	4E	$	41	$	00	$	0C	$	47	$	4E
$	4F	$	4C	$	00	$	4F	$	33	>	A0	50	52	41	43

Life is a mystery, just one big "*what if*?" But the joy is that we alone *set* the direction we choose. Sometimes we may *gain* and sometimes we may *lose*. But with each passing day we're a bit less confused.

---

2 Fair warning—this puzzle is harder than the first two. But if you figure out what the "functions" are, then translate those into pseudocode, you can still solve the problem on paper. Manually walking through each operation will be tedious, so only do that as much needed to check your work.
Writing a program to decode the message will be more efficient, but you will learn more if you gradually disassemble the low-level operations into higher-level functions by hand. Or do both if you'd like. :-)

Acknowledgments

A book is an endless tapestry of hard work, with only part of it weaved by the author. The unique nature of *Programming Beyond Practices* has made it especially dependent on the support and contributions of others, and there is no way I would have been able to ship it on my own.

First and foremost, I want to thank you. This book is meant to serve its readers well, but you still had to do all the heavy lifting. The fact that you have given me your time and attention is more than I could ever ask for, and I cannot thank you enough.

The work was developed under the watchful eye of not one but three top-notch developmental editors: Jeff Bleiel, Brian MacDonald, and Mike Loukides. Mike convinced me to write this book in the first place, and provided support and feedback throughout the project. Brian helped out in the early stages, and Jeff worked tirelessly with me through the most challenging phase in any writing project: turning a haphazard manuscript into a proper book that's worth reading.

I also am lucky to have had an incredible technical review team, which included Michael Feathers, Nell Shamrell, and Saron Yitbarek, as well as an anonymous participant who provided very helpful feedback. Ward Cunningham also provided some brief but thoughtful notes on an early draft of the work.

Stephanie Morillo, the book's copyeditor, turned an awkward word salad into something worth serving up to you. This weird little book needed someone extraordinarily talented to fill this role—and Stephanie fit the bill perfectly.

Kristen Brown guided the production process for this book with an extreme level of precision, care, and patience. This was one of the things I had been most worried about when I set out to write this book, but my fears quickly went away as soon as we started working together.

Despite its small size, this book is the product of thousands of conversations and shared experiences I've had with hundreds of thoughtful and generous people throughout the world. Below I've acknowledged a few dozen of them, but know that it is only a partial list of people who helped bring this work about:

Ben Berkowitz • Sarah Bray • Florian Breisch • Melle Boersma • Ben Callaway • Christian Carter • Joseph Caudle • Mel Conway • Kenn Costales • Liam Dawson • Donovan Dikaio • Brad Ediger • Martin Fowler • Gregory Gibson • Melissa Gibson • Eric Gjersten • James Gifford • James Edward Gray II • David Haslem • Brian Hughes • Ron Jeffries • Alex Kashko • Kam Lasater • Tristan Lescut • Alexander Mankuta • Joseph McCormick • Steve Merrick • Alan Moore • Matthew Nelson • Carol Nichols • Calinoiu Alexandru Nicolae • Stephen Orr • Bruce Park • Srdjan Pejic • Vanja Radovanovic • Donald Reinertsen • Pito Salas • Clive Seebregts • Evan Sharp • Kathy Sierra • Derek Sivers • Danya Smith • Hunter Stevens • Jacob Tjørnholm • Gary Vaynerchuk • Jim Weirich • Solomon White • Jia Wu • Jan Žák

A handful of the people listed above have inspired me indirectly through their own work, but the vast majority have spent some significant time talking with me about ideas and projects that inspired the topics I've spent the last year of my life researching and writing about.

Last but certainly not least, I'd like to thank everyone else on staff at O'Reilly Media who had a hand in creating this book, and Tim O'Reilly for creating an excellent publishing company in the first place. This was a strange and difficult little project, but I was given all the support I needed and then some to bring it to market.

O'Reilly Media, Inc.

Safari® Books Online

 *Safari Books Online* is an on-demand digital library that delivers expert content in both book and video form from the world's leading authors in technology and business.

Technology professionals, software developers, web designers, and business and creative professionals use Safari Books Online as their primary resource for research, problem solving, learning, and certification training. Safari Books Online offers a range of plans and pricing for enterprise, government, education, and individuals.

Members have access to thousands of books, training videos, and prepublication manuscripts in one fully searchable database from publishers like O'Reilly Media, Prentice Hall Professional, Addison-Wesley Professional, Microsoft Press, Sams, Que, Peachpit Press, Focal Press, Cisco Press, John Wiley & Sons, Syngress, Morgan Kaufmann, IBM Redbooks, Packt, Adobe Press, FT Press, Apress, Manning, New Riders, McGraw-Hill, Jones & Bartlett, Course Technology, and hundreds more. For more information about Safari Books Online, please visit us online.

How to Contact Us

Please address comments and questions concerning this book to the publisher:

O'Reilly Media, Inc.
1005 Gravenstein Highway North
Sebastopol, CA 95472
800-998-9938 (in the United States or Canada)
707-829-0515 (international or local)
707-829-0104 (fax)

We have a web page for this book, where we list errata, examples, and any additional information. You can access this page at *http://bit.ly/programming-beyond-practices*.

To comment or ask technical questions about this book, send email to *bookquestions@oreilly.com*.

For more information about our books, courses, conferences, and news, see our website at *http://www.oreilly.com*.

Find us on Facebook: *http://facebook.com/oreilly*

Follow us on Twitter: *http://twitter.com/oreillymedia*

Watch us on YouTube: *http://www.youtube.com/oreillymedia*

Index

implementation of minimal slice of, 61-64
wireframe diagrams for setting expectations
about, 2-4
future issues, 107-116

G

gradual process improvement
as antidote for overcommitment, 91-106
economic tradeoffs, 95-98
identification/analysis of operational bottlenecks, 94
making whole greater than sum of parts,
102-105
unexpected failures, 92-94
waste reduction by limiting work in progress, 98-102

H

hidden abstractions, 71-72
hidden dependencies
avoiding non-essential real-time data syn-
chronization, 26-27
code reuse in new context, 27-29
fallacy of standalone features, 22
in incremental changes, 21-30
of two features on a screen, 23-27
HTML tags, as potential trouble source, 28

I

incremental changes, hidden dependencies in,
21-30
incremental process improvement (see gradual
process improvement)
input data validation, 48-50
integration of external services (see service
integrations)
issue trackers, 95

J

journal, educational, 31-42
just-in-time workflow, software simulation of,
60-73

K

knowledge base, incorporating wiki into, 21-30

L

live test system, 4-6
login systems, failure of, 34-36

M

maintenance
and fallacy of purely internal concerns, 40
problems from poorly coded robots, 38-40
mentoring, programming puzzles as part of,
43-57
mistakes, rapid prototyping, 7-8
mock objects, outdated, 36-38
modeling of data (see data modeling)
music video recommendations system, 1-18

N

needs
of project, 2
unique, as source of trouble, 32-34

O

objects, temporal coupling between, 64-67
operational bottlenecks, 94
overcommitment, gradual process improvement as antidote for (see gradual process
improvement)

P

pain points
in "rose, bud, and thorn" exercise, 102
of service integrations, 31-42
physical modeling, conceptual modeling and,
76-78
problem solving
careful description of problem, 44
checking work with deductive reasoning,
51-52
developing rigorous approach to, 43-57
solving simple problems to understand
more difficult ones, 52-56
validation of input data, 48-50
working problem by hand before writing
code, 46-48
product development, process improvement in
(see gradual process improvement)
production codebase, extension to fit new purpose, 21
production systems, prototypes vs., 13

About the Author

Gregory Brown has run the independently published *Practicing Ruby* journal since 2010, and is the original author of the popular Prawn PDF generation library.

In his consulting projects, Gregory works with stakeholders in companies of all sizes to identify core business problems that can be solved with as little code as possible.

Gregory's relentless focus on the 90% of programming work that isn't just writing code is what led him to begin working on *Programming Beyond Practices*.

Colophon

The animal on the cover of *Programming Beyond Practices* is a Peruvian spider monkey (*Ateles chamek*), also known as a black-faced spider monkey. Despite its name, this primate can be found in Brazil and Bolivia in addition to Peru. It lives in lowland forests, using long limbs and a prehensile tail to swing through the upper canopy with remarkable agility.

The Peruvian spider monkey is a slender animal with dark fur and a black face. Males and females are generally the same size, with an average weight of 15–20 pounds and length of 24 inches (not counting the tail, which can add up to 36 more inches). They are well equipped for life in the treetops, with elongated fingers, a highly flexible shoulder joint, and a partially hairless tail tip that provides a stronger grip on branches. The spider monkey's diet is largely made up of fruit, supplemented with leaves, insects, eggs, honey, and small animals like birds or frogs.

As with most primates, Peruvian spider monkeys live in social groups. The size of the group can change seasonally, as females leave to give birth and return a few months later. Newborn spider monkeys become independent at around 10 months of age, but are not sexually mature until they are 4 years old. These are very vocal animals, with calls that include screams, barks, and horse-like whinnies. They also signal each other by swinging their arms and shaking tree branches.

Like many species native to the rainforest, the Peruvian spider monkey is endangered. Beyond the loss of habitat caused by logging and agricultural activity, it and other large animals are overhunted for the Amazonian bushmeat trade.

Many of the animals on O'Reilly covers are endangered; all of them are important to the world. To learn more about how you can help, go to *animals.oreilly.com*.

The cover image is from a loose plate, source unknown. The cover fonts are URW Typewriter and Guardian Sans. The text font is Adobe Minion Pro; the heading font is Adobe Myriad Condensed; and the code font is Dalton Maag's Ubuntu Mono.

Get even more for your money.

Join the O'Reilly Community, and register the O'Reilly books you own. It's free, and you'll get:

- $4.99 ebook upgrade offer
- 40% upgrade offer on O'Reilly print books
- Membership discounts on books and events
- Free lifetime updates to ebooks and videos
- Multiple ebook formats, DRM FREE
- Participation in the O'Reilly community
- Newsletters
- Account management
- 100% Satisfaction Guarantee

Signing up is easy:

1. Go to: oreilly.com/go/register
2. Create an O'Reilly login.
3. Provide your address.
4. Register your books.

Note: English-language books only

To order books online:
oreilly.com/store

For questions about products or an order:
orders@oreilly.com

To sign up to get topic-specific email announcements and/or news about upcoming books, conferences, special offers, and new technologies:
elists@oreilly.com

For technical questions about book content:
booktech@oreilly.com

To submit new book proposals to our editors:
proposals@oreilly.com

O'Reilly books are available in multiple DRM-free ebook formats. For more information:
oreilly.com/ebooks

O'REILLY®

CPSIA information can be obtained
at www.ICGtesting.com
Printed in the USA
BVOW11s1838091016
464390BV00004B/5/P